This work is dedicated to the memory of
Ray Edward Toms (1922-1969) and of
Tawat Chotigeat (1921-1975).

ACKNOWLEDGMENTS

Any project of this magnitude is not executed as a solo effort, but rather it represents the contribution of many to its success. To those below, I offer my most heartfelt appreciation:

Dr. Clemens L. Hallman, whom I have known since 1986 and who shared his enthusiasm about this project early on in the process, for his continual support and encouragement.

Dr. Sebastian L. Foti, who always had the time to listen and share his thoughts, even when he knew me as no more than a stranger when I first arrived on campus, and who demonstrated his unfailing loyalty throughout the course of my studies.

Dr. James J. Algina for his kind guidance and endless patience as I attempted to gain some mastery of statistical analysis which includes skills similar to those of learning a foreign language--holding many rules in mind simultaneously.

Dr. Richard D. Downie for his assurance and the wisdom of his many years on this campus and in the field of international education.

Dr. Constance L. Shehan for showing early on her willingness to encourage this undertaking and for offering the resources of the University Center for Excellence in Teaching in support of this project.

Tosporn Chotigeat for not wanting me to go but not wanting to hold me back either and for understanding why I wanted to do this.

Ruth Evelyn Bishop Toms King for always telling me that I could do anything that I set my mind to.

TABLE OF CONTENTS

LIST OF TABLES

Abstract of Dissertation Presented to the Graduate School
of the University of Florida in Partial Fulfillment of the
Requirements for the Degree of Doctor of Philosophy

INSTRUCTIONAL USE OF THE INTERNET:
STAGES OF CONCERN AMONG FACULTY
AT THE UNIVERSITY OF FLORIDA

By

Sue Anne Toms

August 1997

Chairman: Clemens L. Hallman
Major Department: Instruction and Curriculum

This descriptive correlational study explored the

patterns in the stages of concern of the faculty at the

University of Florida regarding the innovation adoption of

the Internet for instructional purposes. Recent

technological developments in computers and

telecommunications, especially in access to the storage and

transfer of vast quantities of information, have included

many possibilities for direct application to university

classrooms.

Three research questions were posed. What are the

relationships of the level of Internet use for instructional

purposes and the level of Internet use for all other

purposes to the sequence of stages of concern? Are there

significant differences in the peak stages of concern of the faculty members grouped by the extent to which they modify their instructional practices based on how or what students learn? Are there significant differences in the peak stages of concern among faculty members grouped by rank, gender, age, or national origin.

The Concerns-Based Adoption Model provided the theoretical framework for the study. Made up of several dimensions, CBAM's seven stages of concern represent a developmental sequence through which an individual passes when confronted with change or innovation. The stages range from non-concern (Awareness), to self (Information, Personal), task (Management), and impact concerns (Consequence, Collaboration, and Refocusing).

During Spring 1997 the Stages of Concern Questionnaire was mailed to 1,650 faculty members within ten colleges at the University of Florida. The final sample contained 540 responses, a return rate of 33%. The data were analyzed using correlational and regression techniques.

Findings included significant correlations between the peak or most intense stage of concern and level of use of the Internet for instructional purposes, level of use of the Internet for all other purposes, and attention to how students learn. However, the multiple regression model produced only two significant predictors of peak stage of concern: level of use of the Internet for instructional

purposes and gender.

CHAPTER 1
INTRODUCTION

*The history of modern education is littered with
the trash of technology left behind by unrealistic
purchases, naive users, and vendors working on a
quota system.* (Polley, 1977, cited in Albright,
1996, p. 2)

Statement of the Problem

This quantitative study explored the patterns in the
needs thoughts, feelings, and perceptions of the University
of Florida faculty as manifested in their stages of concern
regarding the innovation adoption of the Internet for
instructional purposes. The sources of the problem are
several. The first involves the trend of traditional brick-
and-mortar colleges and universities investigating novel
modes of instructional delivery facilitated by recent
technological developments in computers and
telecommunications. Another stems from the customary
approach to faculty development within these organizations,
one which seldom considers at the level of the individual
the psychological orientation which occurs with expectations
for incorporation of these technological changes into their
daily teaching lives. Finally, the need originates in the

1

current tensions at universities across the nation between incoming students' increasing levels of technological sophistication and their demands for access to computers and networked resources to supplement and enhance their own learning. These tensions place unprecedented strains on ever tighter budgets.

Need for the Study

Current Changes in Institutions of Higher Education

The innovation central to this study, use of the Internet for instructional purposes, stands poised to complement substantially the primacy of the model of higher learning which has prevailed for many centuries in the Western world. The rise of monasteries as centers of learning produced the classroom model as we now know it. Classrooms where an expert gathered with students and talked to them to transmit knowledge represent the oral, pre-print tradition (Warnock, 1996). Same time/same place for teacher and student was the requirement in this transmission model of teaching and learning.

The advent of the printing press brought about repositories of knowledge in the form of libraries where information could be stored through time on the substrate of paper. Thus, students were able to learn from the *written* works of past (even deceased) scholars, but they still had to adhere to the 'same place' requirement, gathering where these libraries were located. Knowledge transmission continued to dominate.

In the present age, both time and place are losing their importance. The availability and distribution of information and with it knowledge are changing drastically. The Internet represents a new medium for the storage and transfer of information, both without the customary substrate of paper (Warnock, 1996). Sources of information distributed throughout networks accessible more widely than ever before are becoming the norm.

Full realization of all that this means to the world of students, scholars, and researchers will not be achieved for some time to come. Nevertheless, the present represents a key moment in the evolution of the spread of knowledge, the likes of which have not been seen for many hundreds of years. This is not to say that the current paradigm will be replaced any time soon nor that it will ever disappear. One fact is unarguable, however; new features will be added. As the president of Harvard recently mused, "The world of learning will not become lost in cyberspace, I suspect, any more than it has drowned in books" (Rudenstine, 1997, p. A48).

Teaching During These Changes

The process of "becoming a teacher is complex, stressful, intimate, and largely covert" (Fuller & Brown, 1975, p. 75). College professors participate in this process and find all of the above amplified. Furthermore, the process is compounded for those who are expected to keep abreast of changes in the teaching of their disciplines and who are interested in incorporating what adoption of instructional innovation offers.

The individuals in the front lines of instructional innovation or change at post-secondary institutions, that is the teaching faculty, are seldom trained in any systematic way to become members of the professorate. They may have taught as graduate students, but they usually have chosen a career in the academic world due to an affinity for their content area or for research. Those who feel a commitment to teaching well and express an interest in improving their teaching skills can typically avail themselves of the campus resources at hand. Among the options at the University of Florida is the University Center for Excellence in Teaching.

UCET's primary mission is to assure access to the resources needed for teaching by both new and established faculty. Its major functions include supplying new faculty with "orientation, instruction, and consultation about teaching and learning" (Shehan, 1994, p. 1). To this end, its Advisory Board members act as consultants or partners to new faculty to facilitate development of their teaching styles and philosophies (Shehan, 1994).

In addition, another charge of UCET is to "[f]acilitate the continuing development of tenured faculty as teachers" (Shehan, 1995, p. 4) The center offers information about developments related to teaching at the higher education level through its *Conversations about Teaching* series and the *Focus on Teaching* annual workshops. Finally, UCET contributes to the preparation of graduate students for their roles as future educators (Shehan, 1995, p. 4).

Two examples of the application of instructional uses of the Internet advocated by UCET are found in a recent issue of the center's newsletter in an article on teaching large classes. The author offers eight suggestions, among them encouraging others to "[d]evelop a homepage so that students can get important information from there rather than calling you" and "[e]ncourage the use of e-mail as a way for students to get their questions answered. That way you can respond at your convenience and save time" (Schwartz, 1996, p. 2).

Although prominent among the topics recently offered in UCET activities are diversity in the classroom and dealing with individual differences in learning styles, Loucks and

Hall (1977) make the valid point that when teachers or faculty are trained in some new instructional innovation, they are often not treated as diverse individuals themselves (p. 18). Faculty development is seldom carried out on the basis of the needs and concerns of the faculty. For staff developers whose clients teach across a myriad of disciplines, in class groups of from 7 to 700, to students who are fresh on the university scene or those who may have been there nearly a decade, making instructional interventions relevant is indeed a challenge.

This study speaks directly to this need. It yields concerns data collected at the level of the individual regarding adoption of the innovation of using the Internet for instructional purposes using the Stages of Concern Questionnaire, part of the Concerns-Based Adoption Model. The model was devised to depict "the process of change in terms of the individuals involved" (Loucks & Hall, 1977, p. 18). Hall and Loucks (1978) list the six basic assumptions that underlie the model: (1) rather than an event, change is a process; (2) facilitating change involves the individual as the "primary target"; (3) change occurs at a very personal level; (4) the change process occurs along a pathway marked by stages in both thoughts and skills; (5) interventions by staff developers are most effective when they focus on the client and follow a "diagnostic/

prescriptive model"; and (6) the effectiveness of staff development will depend on constant diagnostic input and on systematic adaptation of the intervention as well as of the innovation itself (pp. 37-38).

Within the CBAM structure are found basic frames of reference, of which the concerns dimension is one. Concerns have been defined as "perceptions, feelings, and motivations" (Hall & Loucks, 1978, p. 39) which beset an individual faced with change. Interventions based on individuals' concerns not only facilitate the process of adoption of an innovation, they also increase the effectiveness and efficiency of the adoption and decrease the trauma of the change for the individual. In short, information on individuals' stages of concerns provides a powerful tool for improving staff development interventions.

The Institutional Context

The final source of the problem at hand involves the context within which the study was set. Two principal factors constitute the pertinence of the study's outcomes to the conditions regarding adoption of the Internet for instructional purposes at the University of Florida.

The first of these factors revolves around the student-driven movement to assure the accustomed access to and use of the Internet without students incurring additional costs.

Until spring semester 1996 all UF students (even members of
the general public) had access to computer labs on campus
and to the full range of applications and networking offered
without charge. Starting with that semester, however,
undergraduate students were assessed a charge of $20 for
maintenance of an account which included basic Internet
access (they still could use word-processing, spreadsheet
and database applications free of charge). At that point,
the administration made a distinction between what was
considered essential computer access and what was considered
elective, a dichotomy with which the student body could not
agree.

The uproar caused by the imposition of the fee finally
resulted in a November 19, 1996, letter from the UF Student
Senate President to all faculty including the full text of a
resolution passed unanimously by the Senate expressing the
students' view: "the use of computers as an *essential*,
rather than *elective*, element of fulfilling educational
goals" (C. E. Dorworth, communication, November 19, 1996).
In addition, the letter went on to ask that all faculty
include the following in the syllabus for each course they
teach:

It is the formal policy of this class that in
order to fully and properly fulfill the
requirements of this course some use of and
proficiency in the use of computers, including
access to and use of the Internet (e-mail and
World Wide Web), will be required. (C. E.
Dorworth, communication, November 19, 1996)

Clearly, adoption of the innovation of the Internet for
learning purposes among the students represented by their
Student Senate had out paced the ability of the
administration to provide access to it within the given
budgetary constraints. (For full text of letter and
resolution, see Appendix A.)

The tensions fueled by student demands on limited
resources were not unique to the University of Florida
campus; they were also apparent at the level of the (state)
Board of Regents during the fall of 1996 and into 1997.
Despite student protest and after debating proposals as high
as $100, at their meeting on January 24, 1997, the Board
approved a recommendation that the legislature vote to
assess a technology fee of $50 per student throughout the
State University System (Malernee, 1997). This represents a
potential inflow of approximately $2,000,000 in the
technology budget for the University of Florida. Making a
contribution to a well-informed decision on allocation of
this money to avoid the "trash of technology left behind by
. . . naive users" (Polley, 1977, cited in Albright, 1996,

p. 2), as mentioned at the outset, represents the second factor in the significance of the outcomes and the single greatest need for this study.

Research Questions

What are the concerns regarding adoption of the Internet for instructional purposes among the faculty at the University of Florida? To explore this question, the following were answered:

(1) What are the relationships of the level of Internet use for instructional purposes and the level of Internet use for all other purposes to the sequence of stages of concern?

(2) Are there significant differences in the peak stages of concern of the faculty members grouped by the extent to which they modify their instructional practices based on how or what students learn?

(3) Are there significant differences in the peak stages of concern among faculty members grouped by rank, gender, age, or national origin?

Limitations and Assumptions

The findings offer a one-time view of a dynamic process--the respondents' moves through the developmental stages of concern about an innovation. The subjects were instructional faculty affiliated with an academic unit within the ten college-level units which offer undergraduate education at a large southeastern U.S. research university. Generalizibility is limited to those who completed the survey.

The data were collected on a survey undertaken by the University Center for Excellence in Teaching. The quantity and quality of the responses may be influenced by this fact. Those who have had experience with and benefitted from UCET-sponsored activities may have been more likely to reply.

Since response to the questionnaire was voluntary, response rates may have been higher among those with a higher-than-representative degree of interest in and/or experience with use of the Internet for instructional purposes.

The results reflected the respondents' honest concerns and are valid to the extent that the respondents share the definitions of the terms used with those of the researcher.

Definition of Terms

For the purposes of this study, the following definitions have been used:

The <u>Internet</u> is an international network linking smaller networks; it includes electronic mail and file transfer capabilities, as well as access to information (text, graphics, audio, video) throughout those networks (Oblinger, 1992).

Instructional purpose refers to a use (either required or optional) to support classroom routines, e.g., course announcements, distributing hand-outs, sending or receiving assignments, and research for term projects.

Concern is the mental construct represented by an individual's feelings, preoccupations, thoughts, and considerations directed at a specific task to be accomplished or an issue to be resolved. This definition follows that developed by Hall et al. (1979).

Stages of concern constitute a sequential set through which a person passes when confronted with change.

Stages of Concern Questionnaire (SoCQ) is an instrument with thirty-five Likert-type items yielding scores on seven subscales to measure the intensities of concern of educators about the adoption of an educational innovation (Hall et al., 1979).

Peak stage of concern is that stage with the highest score and thus the most intense concern. A given individual may exhibit varying levels of concern on the multiple items measuring within the same stage, but an overall score for each stage will show the stage of greatest intensity. In the event of equal scores on two or more stages, the stage furthest forward on the continuum, and thus in the process of adoption innovation, was used.

Concerns Based Adoption Model (CBAM) is a conceptual framework for understanding how individuals in educational settings react to change. It posits that change is a process, that it occurs at the level of the individual and should therefore be measured at that level, and that individuals confronted with change pass through a developmental sequence of stages of concern as they adopt that change. The stages of concern are one dimension of the model (Hall et al., 1973).

Faculty refers to those persons employed at the University of Florida during spring semester 1997 who are remunerated as faculty within one of the following ten college-level units: Architecture, Business Administration, Education, Engineering, Fine Arts, Health and Human Performance, Health Professions, the Institute of Food and Agricultural Sciences, Journalism and Communications, and Liberal Arts.

Foreign faculty are those of the above group who are not native-born American citizens. They may be naturalized American citizens, permanent residents, or holders of a visa which permits them to work in the United States.

CHAPTER 2
REVIEW OF THE LITERATURE

The literature review for this study opens with a summary of the findings of the two antecedents to the theoretical framework central to it--research on the adoption and diffusion of innovations and on beginning teachers' concerns. It then turns to the Concerns-Based Adoption Model, explaining its various dimensions and tracing the development of the first one, Stages of Concern. Examples of models which have incorporated the CBAM are given. The review continues with a close look at the survey instrument which measures the first dimension, the Stages of Concern Questionnaire, including how it was developed and its psychometric properties. This is followed by a review of the literature concerning the variables captured on the demographic page which makes up part of the instrument used for this study. Finally, the research on current practices of using the Internet for instructional purposes in higher education settings is reviewed.

Adoption and Diffusion of Innovations

Within the vast body of research and theory on innovation adoption, of direct relevance to this study is the work of Everett Rogers. By synthesizing the findings and theories from over 500 publications in his 1962 work Diffusion of Innovations, he made a lasting contribution to this area and significantly added to what is known about adoption of an innovation.

The basic elements of diffusion of any innovation are (a) the innovation, (b) its communication from one individual to another, (c) the social system, and (d) a period of time (Rogers, 1962, p. 12). While diffusion operates at the level of the social system or across systems, adoption as a process does so at the level of the individual. Rogers (1962) defines adoption as "the mental process through which an individual passes from first hearing about an innovation to final adoption" (p. 17). Rogers segmented the adoption process into five stages: awareness, interest, evaluation, trial, and adoption. Through these five stages, the individual moves from a point of random exposure to the innovation, to actively seeking information about it, weighing its possible benefits, trying it out on a limited basis, and finally adopting it. Although rejection may truncate the process at any stage, the outcome of the fourth stage (trial) is crucial to moving to the final stage (pp. 81-86).

Rogers also typified adopters by the sequence in which they adopt an innovation and their salient characteristics. He termed those at the lead in the process "innovators" who are venturesome; the next group are called "early adopters" and are respected by others; the following "early majority" are deliberate; the "late majority" are skeptics; and the final "laggards" are traditional (Rogers, 1962, pp. 168-171).

Beginning Teacher Concerns

Central to Frances Fuller's research (1969) was an exploration of the mental processes of an individual who is confronted with change manifested in the demands of learning to practice a future profession. Her pioneering studies on undergraduate education majors dealing with the mismatch between (a) their own motivation to learn and (b) the content and sequence of the academic courses that teacher educators had deemed appropriate and necessary for them (1969) have made a lasting contribution.

To improve the match between learner goals and teacher preparation programs, more information was needed about the concerns of future teachers. An analysis of previous studies about beginning teachers' concerns revealed surprisingly consistent patterns, although missing were concerns over the topics covered in the typical undergraduate teacher-training curriculum (Fuller, 1969, pp. 208-210).

During counseling sessions with student teachers in Fuller's first study, two categories of concerns emerged: those with the self and those with pupils. Furthermore, the preponderance of topics in the two categories was not scattered about randomly during the eleven weeks of counseling sessions, but rather a developmental pattern from self to pupils was uncovered. In her second study, written responses to open-ended concerns statements with student teachers lent validity to the self-other dichotomy and its sequential attribute. By reviewing findings of previous studies through this 'dichotomous' lens, as well as by looking at (then) contemporary unpublished data from colleagues, Fuller found further support for the two categories and their developmental nature (1969).

Attempts to categorize the "amorphous and vague" responses about concerns from education majors *before* their student teaching experience, i.e., during their sophomore and junior years, proved more elusive (Fuller, 1969, p. 219). As a result, a pre-teaching phase with non-concern was added at the front of the two-phase developmental model

of teacher concerns conceptualized as self-->other. Among
the implications for further research, Fuller questions the
validity of generalization to other groups, including
college professors, and the feasibility of developing an
instrument for measuring concerns, thus opening the way to
her successors.

The timelessness of Fuller's findings is demonstrated
by the appearance of articles decades later exploring the
development of professors' careers as teachers. Kugel
(1993) proposes three major stages that professors move
through as they hone their teaching abilities. The first
centers on the self, the second on the subject matter at
hand, and the third on the student. The parallel between
such a model and the self-->other model of Fuller is
evident.

The Concerns-Based Adoption Model

While the legacy left by Rogers's work was much
knowledge in understanding innovation diffusion and adoption
at the level of social interaction and that of Fuller was a
glance into the motivation, thoughts, feelings, and
perceptions of beginning teachers, the Concerns-Based
Adoption Model or CBAM developed by Gene Hall and his
associates had as its mission "the study of what happens to
the individual classroom teacher and professor involved in

change" (Hall, 1976, p. 22). The CBAM, in conjunction with the Procedures for Adopting Educational Innovations Project at The Research and Development Center for Teacher Education, University of Texas, addresses innovation adoption within an educational setting not as an event, but rather as a long-term process from the perspectives of the individual, the organization, and the innovation (Hall et al., 1975; Loucks & Hall, 1977). Goals of the model include describing developmental changes in individuals as they move through the process and effective intervention strategies which can facilitate that movement. The basic diagnostic frame of reference in the model includes the dimensions of (a) the concerns that users have prior to and during adoption of an innovation (Stages of Concern), (b) the way in which the innovation is actually used (Levels of Use), and (c) how the innovation itself adapts to the exigencies of the adopters (Innovation Configuration). In addition, the fourth component prescribes intervention parameters to facilitate the change process (Intervention Taxonomy and Intervention Anatomy) (Hord & Loucks, 1980).

Stages of Concern

The CBAM project identified seven stages of concern about an innovation (SoC). These stages expand on those first proposed by Fuller and are grouped into self, task, and impact concerns. Concerns are considered to be manifestations of what an individual involved in the change process is feeling, a construct referring "to the categorization of expressions stated by the user related to his use of the innovation" (Hall et al., 1973, p. 14). Originally, the seven stages of concern were described as (0) unaware, (1) awareness, (2) exploration, (3) early trial, (4) limited impact, (5) maximum benefit, and (6) renewal (Hall et al., 1973). Whereas the original works had identified the concerns of preservice teachers, Hall (1976) presents findings derived from a study that included inservice teachers and professors in college settings. Additional research resulted in defining the concerns more precisely, developing a measurement of the stages of concern, and testing the concerns across innovations (Hall & Rutherford, 1976; Hall et al., 1977). Additional applications of the concerns model to the change process are reported among university administrators, state education agency officials, and those working in the private sector (Hall, 1979, 1985). Refined definitions of the stages of concern (from Hall et al., 1979 [original concept from Hall et al., 1973]) are given as

Non-concern--0 Awareness. Little concern about or involvement with the innovation is indicated.

Self--1 Informational. A general awareness of the
innovation and interest in learning more detail about it is
indicated. The person seems to be unworried about
himself/herself in relation to the innovation. S/he is
interested in substantive aspects of the innovation in a
selfless manner such as general characteristics, effects,
and requirements for use.

2 Personal. Individual is uncertain about the demands
of the innovation, his/her inadequacy to meet those
demands, and his/her role with the innovation. This
includes analysis of his/her role in relation to the reward
structure of the organization, decision making, and
consideration of potential conflicts with existing
structures or personal commitment. Financial or status
implications of the program for self and colleagues may also
be reflected.

Task--3 Management. Attention is focused on the
processes and tasks of using the innovation and the best use
of information and resources. Issues related to efficiency,
organizing, managing, scheduling, and time demands are
utmost.

Impact--4 Consequence. Attention focuses on impact of
the innovation on student in his/her immediate sphere of
influence. The focus is on relevance of the innovation for
students, evaluation of student outcomes, including

performance and competencies, and changes needed to increase student outcomes.

5 Collaboration. The focus is on coordination and cooperation with others regarding use of the innovation.

6 Refocusing. The focus is on exploration of more universal benefits from the innovation, including the possibility of major changes or replacement with a more powerful alternative. Individual has definite ideas about alternatives to the proposed or existing form of the innovation.

Levels of Use

The second diagnostic component of the CBAM, levels of use of the innovation, explains actual behaviors of the innovation user without regard to such affective variables as attitudes, motivation, or needs (those which are central to the stages of concern) (Hall et al., 1975, p. 52). In the broadest sense, stages of concern move from self to task to impact whereas levels of use follow an orienting to managing to integrating path (Loucks & Hall, 1977). The eight levels of use describe the behaviors of the user (as opposed to the feelings of the stages of concern) ranging from non-use to orientation, preparation, mechanical use, routine, refinement, integration, and renewal (Hall et al.,

1975; Loucks & Hall, 1977). These levels have been compared to those passed through by a person learning to drive an automobile (Hall & Hord, 1987, pp. 17-18). Assessment of individuals' stages of concern and levels of use is considered essential to choosing appropriate modes of intervention in order to maximize the effectiveness and efficiency of the change process and minimize the trauma of that process on the individual. Interventions must be coordinated with adopters' levels of use to be of maximum benefit (Hall et al., 1975, p. 56). In addition, multiple cycles of use make up the innovation adoption process and intervention support must fall across these cycles.

Hall and Hord (1984) discuss the complex relationship between stages of concern and levels of use, stating that at the two extremes there seems to be a positive, linear relationship, i.e. an individual whose peak stage of concern falls at or near either extreme of the seven-unit SoC continuum will tend to also be at or near that same extreme level of use on the eight-unit LoU continuum. The relationship between the two dimensions for those who fall in the middle on one or both, nevertheless, is much less clear. The overall hypothesized relationship follows an elongated S-curve where "at early points in the change process, use tends to 'drive' concerns, and at later points, aroused concerns push Levels of Use" (Hall & Hord, 1984, p. 338).

Innovation Configuration

The third diagnostic dimension of the CBAM model involves clarifying and operationalizing what use of the innovation in its intended setting means (Hall & Loucks, 1981). The Innovation Configuration acknowledges an interaction between the innovation user and the innovation itself. By means of a checklist, it assesses user patterns from among the components a user may or may not choose to adopt. Each individual has a unique 'fingerprint' which shows the pattern of that person's encounter with the innovation. It will include the components selected, their organization, and their variations (Yessayan, 1991). Implications for change facilitators are clear; once acceptable components and variations have been identified, guiding users along the path of adoption is greatly simplified. In addition, adopters evaluate their progress and gauge the distance left to complete the change process. Rutherford outlines the categories of components to an innovation configuration: those which are crucial to the innovation (musts), those which are desirable, and those which are suitable but not required (1986, pp. 10-13).

Intervention Taxonomy (IT) and Intervention Anatomy (IA)

Later research on the CBAM has resulted in a final two-part dimension which must also be mentioned. With an eye toward more effective interventions for the successful adoption of an innovation, the Intervention Taxonomy and Intervention Anatomy were developed. The IT facilitates comprehensive intervention planning by specifying six levels for school improvement and staff development. The IA addresses the internal components of potential interventions and yields information which, when used with the IT, contributes to more effectively addressing the individuals' needs (Hord & Loucks, 1980).

Change Facilitator Stages of Concern and Questionnaire

A more recent addition to the body of theory and instruments to grow out of the original CBAM is the Change Facilitator Stages of Concern dimension and its corresponding CFSoC Questionnaire. Administration of the original SoCQ to those charged with managing or facilitating change proved inappropriate. For example, educational supervisors are typically not concerned about use of the innovation as adopters (teachers) are but rather with realizing their role in helping the adopters use the innovation. As a result, the CFSoCQ was developed (Hall et al., 1991).

This instrument was used at the beginning and end of a one-month residential training program for secondary school science department heads in the Philippines during the summer of 1991. Since the administrative structure of educational authority places responsibility for instructional leadership with these individuals, their role is that of change facilitator within their own schools (Matthews, 1993). The change facilitator concerns data collected at the beginning was used to aid in the design of the staff development program. Post-program data on the change facilitator participants' stages of concern showed significant progress through the developmental stages.

Models Incorporating the Concerns-Based Adoption Model

Building on CBAM for the enhancement of staff development interventions, McCarthy (1982) has included the stages of concern in her novel approach to teacher inservice. Starting with modes of perception from thinking to sensing/feeling along one axis, and adding modes of processing from doing to watching along another axis, she derives the four major learning styles. She then dissects each learning style quadrant into two halves to portray right-brain/left-brain dominance, and finally superimposes the seven stages of concern (the first six inside the now circular diagram and the seventh--refocusing--leaving the circle). Her trademarked system called 4Mat accounts for the affective stages of concern and guides a staff developer to meeting the "needs of all four major learning styles, while using right and left mode techniques" (McCarthy, 1982, p. 20).

The stages of concern of the CBAM have also been proposed in a model for faculty development specifically aimed at technological innovations (Wedman & Strathe, 1985). The authors advocate diverse strategies of faculty development derived from three dimensions: the concerns dimension (which they have simplified into four levels-- information, exploration, utilization, and collaboration/innovation), the organization dimension (individual, groups, departments, college), and the faculty context dimension (instructional, creative, management, personal). The result is a framework which may serve as an alternative to the traditional "spray and pray" (Wedman & Strathe, 1985, p. 19) approach to faculty development.

The usefulness of applying data from the first two diagnostic dimensions of the Concerns-Based Adoption Model to the design of inservice training is demonstrated in a

series of articles by Cicchelli and Baecher. Their 1987
work reports on 18 senior high school teachers undergoing
inservice regarding the use of microcomputers in the
classroom. Data gleaned from the stages of concern
questionnaire and levels of use interviews (of three users
and three non-users) served to guide the design and
implementation of 15 hours of training over three days.
Post-training administration of the SoCQ showed "a
significant change in teachers' concerns towards
microcomputers" (p. 85). In a similar study also involving
the implementation of computer technology at the high school
level, six teachers filled out the SoCQ to supply
information used in a nine-hour inservice program. When
administered the SoCQ afterward, the teachers showed a
difference of at least 10 percentile points in each stage
score (1990).

Cicchelli (1990) enlisted stages of concern theory when
confronted anew with Fuller's conundrum of some two decades
before about the best content and sequence of courses for
teacher education programs. The Fordham University Pre-
Service Program enrolls both fourth-year undergraduate and
fifth-year graduate students in a year of
professional/technical teacher training. The difference
between the two groups is in the additional training in

liberal arts which the fifth-year students have had. The SoCQ was administered to 24 fourth-year and 17 fifth-year students at the beginning and again at the end of the two-semester preservice program. Liberal arts training as a part of teacher preparation programs would be supported if the fifth-year students were found to be further along in the developmental sequence of stages of concern at the beginning or at the end of their year of professional teacher training, i.e., if they demonstrated lower self concerns and/or higher impact concerns. This, however, was not the case when looking at the two groups. At least on the personal dimension of concerns about teaching, the additional training in liberal arts cannot be linked to a more advanced starting point on or greater movement along the SoC wave-like pattern either before or after a one-year program of professional/technical education training (Cicchelli, 1990, p. 45).

The Stages of Concern Questionnaire

The stages of concern are assessed on a questionnaire of thirty-five items where respondents indicate the relevance of the statements to their present concerns regarding an innovation. Use of the SoCQ results in "standardized, individualized data that can be aggregated and used to facilitate, monitor, plan, and communicate about a change process" (Hall & Hord, 1987, p. 333). This questionnaire was developed and copyrighted in 1974 by The Research and Development Center for Teacher Education at The University of Texas at Austin as part of the Procedures for Adopting Educational Innovations/CBAM Project (Hall et al., 1979).

Development of the Stages of Concern Questionnaire

The conceptual basis for developing a questionnaire of concerns about adoption of an innovation grew out of the extensive work of Fuller and others during the 1960s. To develop this "quick-scoring, paper-pencil instrument" (Hall & Rutherford, 1976, p. 228), Hall and his associates elicited responses to an open-ended concerns statement, forced rankings, Likert scales, adjective checklists, and interviews; and from a total of 544 Q-sorted items, a group of 400 were judged as central (by a minimum of six out of ten judges) to the measurement of the seven concerns derived from the definitions espoused in the original 1973 CBAM paper (Hall et al., 1973, 1979, p. 9). From these, editing and eliminating redundant items left 195.

Hall and Rutherford (1976) report on the administration of the 195-item pilot instrument to elementary teachers

involved with teaming and college faculty involved with
instructional modules (each group's members stratified by
their length of experience with the innovation in hopes of
capturing information from people all along the full
continuum of stages). Data from the 366 respondents were
factor analyzed, and the first seven resulting factors were
found to be congruent with the outcome of the previous Q-
sort. The resultant 35 items were produced when the factors
were rotated in the direction of the originally defined
stages (factor loadings exceeding 0.5) (Hall & Rutherford,
1976). Between 1974 and 1976, the shortened instrument was
administered to educators involved with eleven different
innovations for results in both cross-sectional and
longitudinal studies (Hall et al., 1979).

Psychometric Properties

The reliability of the SoCQ is interpreted from the
reported test-retest correlations for each of the seven
stages (n = 132, two weeks elapsed) of from 0.65 to 0.86
(four of the seven correlations were above 0.80) (Hall et
al., 1979). The alpha coefficients of internal reliability
of the stages for the same group range from 0.80 to 0.93
(Hall & Rutherford, 1976). Data from a stratified sample of
teachers and professors numbering 830, however, show alpha

coefficients for the seven stages of from 0.64 to 0.83 (six of the seven correlations above 0.70)(Hall et al., 1979).

Indications of the validity of concerns theory and the instrument include a report of the correlations between individual items and the stage which they supposedly measure (72% of the items had higher correlations with their assigned stage than with other stages), lower correlations between distant stages than between adjacent ones, results of factor analyses which indicate independence of the individual stage subscales, and multi-method procedures using the open-ended concerns statements, surveys, and interviews--all resulting in multiple Rs greater than .56 (p < .05) for four of the seven stages--and longitudinal studies demonstrating the wave-like pattern of movement through the stages (Hall et al., 1979).

The 1979 manual for scoring and interpreting the SoCQ calls to the attention of the potential user of the instrument a few of its limitations. First among these is the purpose of its use; having been devised for diagnostic functions, Hall et al. (1979) point out that any use which might involve "screening or evaluation" or even judgement about personality would be inappropriate (p. 57). Secondly, the age group on which the instrument was normed was adult, and their occupational affiliations were with educational institutions; use of the SoCQ with persons outside these groups would invalidate the claims of reliability and validity. Finally, the quality of the results of the analyses is dependent on the good will of the respondents as they fill out the questionnaire.

The Demographic Data Page

In addition to the thirty-five items designed to gather data on the concerns of the individual respondents to the SoCQ, a demographic data page is also included. The information collected from the responses to these items serves a two-fold purpose: description of the survey sample and comparison of it to the population and input for statistical analyses.

Results of research reported by Hall et al. (1979) report "no outstanding relationships between standard demographic variables and concerns data" (p. 52). One of his associates, William Rutherford, concurs by mentioning age, gender, and years of teaching experience as lacking any "consistent relationship" between them and concerns stages scores (1986, p. 7).

In their research article on student engagement of 90 developmental reading students at El Camino College, Marsh and Penn (1988) also report no relationship between stages

of concern and demographic variables. Numerous other
studies report no significant differences in SoC scores
according to demographic variables (Shoemaker, 1990; Falvo,
1990; Hickox, 1994; Lewis, 1994).

Exception to the lack of findings related to age is
taken by Lee-Kang (1993), who found that undergraduate
textiles, clothing, and merchandising program departments
with a greater number of males over sixty were associated
with a lesser degree of adoption of the instructional use of
computers.

A study by Wells and Anderson (1995) which looked into
the relationship between gender (and various levels of
computer knowledge) and SoC scores before, during, and after
a course called Computers and Telecommunications in
Education for graduate students majoring in education at
West Virginia University found that gender was associated
with significant differences at the final administration of
the questionnaire on Stage 0 Awareness and at the midpoint
administration for Stage 5 Collaboration and Stage 6
Refocusing. However, since details about the sample size
and gender breakdown are not reported, these findings are
difficult to evaluate.

A review of the research on the variables of rank and
tenure also finds claims on both sides of the innovation

adoption. King (1990) claims that "junior faculty work on instructional innovation at their peril" (p. 297), yet Lee-Kang in the 1993 study cited above found that more assistant professors in a program increased the likelihood of implementation of instructional computer use at higher levels.

In contrast to the standard demographic variables, those which make up the constellation termed the "state of the user system" by Hall et al. (1979) seem to be more crucial to a full understanding of the stages of concern framework. Among these, the most prominent is the second diagnostic dimension of the CBAM, levels of use.

Also comprising the set of variables defining the 'state of the user system' are the length of time the user has had experience with the innovation and whether the user has had any formal training in the innovation. Both experience and training have been found to be significantly related to SoC in a number of studies. Aneke (1996) found that high school teachers in Virginia involved with the High Schools That Work reform had SoC that correlated positively with the amount of experience with and number of hours of training in the innovation. McQuain (1995) polled teachers at thirteen high schools and a community college in Virginia about the innovation of Technical Preparation (Tech Prep) programs and found both experience and training to be significantly related to SoC. Chandler (1994) researched the innovation of institutional effectiveness criteria in North Carolina community colleges and found significant differences in respondents grouped by level of (a) experience and (b) training.

While exploring how innovative instructional computer users in the School of Humanities and Sciences at Stanford differed from their colleagues, Leong-Childs (1989) found that how professors conceptualized their role as teachers was important in explaining these patterns. Those who paid more attention to *how* their students learn (whom she deemed transactive teachers) had a significantly higher probability of using computers in innovative instructional ways than those who primarily attended to *what* their students learn (transmissive teachers).

Finally, Shoemaker (1990) explored the relationship between differences on SoC scores regarding innovative computer use and native language and culture among foreign-born faculty members in ten foreign language departments at the Defense Language Institute. The ten language groups differed significantly on four of the seven SoC, and he thus concluded that culture (defined by native language and country of birth) plays a significant role in types and intensity of concerns about the innovation of instructional computer use at DLI.

Instructional Use of the Internet in Higher Education

From its originally conceived role as crucial to national security, the Internet has undergone several transformations (Dankel, 1996). Its defense role led to greater dispersion among a select community of university scholars and researchers for sharing and collaborating on government-funded projects. Further development permitted greater spread throughout academic institutions and greatly increased numbers of users. Under the Internet umbrella and spurning on its growth is the World Wide Web, developed in 1989 at CERN, the European Laboratory for Particle Physics. The release in November, 1992, of a new tool, the Mosaic web browser, made searching much easier and thus opened the door for users with less computer acumen (Dankel, 1996). Subsequent additions of user-friendly browsers have continued the trend.

In summing up the year of 1993 and what happened in networking at institutions of higher education, Clement and Abrahams (1994) also give a taxonomy of instructional uses of the Internet at that point in time:

In postsecondary settings, trends are for gradually
increasing use of networking to support education, in
contrast with research, where networking is well
established and near-essential in many disciplines. An
underlying trend that leads to ongoing change is the
pervasive invasion of campus networks into the college
culture at many universities. We see collaborative
courses being taught by faculty, often between
campuses; we see professors offering network bulletin
boards as course discussion areas, offering tutorial
chat lines and e-mail addresses at the equivalent of
"office hours"; assignment delivery via networks; and
network-based projects and simulations used as course
laboratory areas. The frequency of these applications,
though increasing, is still small in relation to the
total of campus opportunities. (p. 107)

Green's (1996) exhaustive, annual campus computing

survey of two- and four-year public and private colleges and

universities gives the reader a comprehensive view. The

data collected during fall 1995 from the 645 respondents

(survey sent to the primary academic computing official at

each of the 1,500 institutions in the sample), including 42

public research universities which most resemble the

institution of this study, show that approximately 75% of

all faculty have access to the Internet, although only 6% of

all college courses make use of resources on the World Wide

Web for instructional support (Green, 1996, p. 15). Further

indication of this small but growing trend is evidenced by

71.5% of the respondents rating Internet resources for

instruction as a "very important" priority and 50.3% also

seeing web pages for individual classes or whole courses at

the same level of importance in the coming 2-3 years (p. 2).
Nevertheless, only 15% of universities reported having a
plan in place for incorporation of instructional resources
drawn from the Internet/World Wide Web (p. 8). Finally,
97.4% of the respondents agreed fully or agreed somewhat
that over the next 2-3 years the Internet/World Wide Web
will be an "important source for content and instructional
resources" (p. 18).

Maddux's 1994 article dealing with seven different
prospects and the problems of adopting the Internet as an
instructional innovation cautions the reader about
statistics such as those above, particularly with regard to
'access.' While a figure like 75% of all faculty with
Internet 'access' may seem to pave the way for fairly rapid
incorporation of its resources into instruction, Maddux
points out that what is often termed 'access' is mere
physical availability. He says that instructional access to
the benefits of an information technology such as the
Internet is something much more complex. Another of his
stated problems involves support for adoption of the
Internet as an innovation. Support must be of two kinds:
technical and curriculum. It is precisely this curriculum
support which is the typically missing link between

availability of a new technology and access to its instructional potential.

Discipline-specific accounts of experiences with the development of instructional uses of the Internet abound. Some, such as Smith's 1995 article, provide insights into new ways of communicating in both directions between instructor and student as well as student and student in a particular discipline (physics in this case), but applications are easily imagined across disciplines. Others explore how teaching college-level writing is changing and is changed by use of the Internet, and still others present specific case studies including the new skills which are added and the wider range of materials such as hypertext documents, all despite the typically "chilly embrace humanities departments have given computers" (Rouzie, 1995, p. 4).

Some accounts are more than personal histories, as teachers look for empirical evidence of differences in student learning as a result of integrating use of the Internet into their courses. A professor of sociology at California State University at Northridge randomly divided his Fall 1996 class in statistics, assigning one group to his accustomed format and teaching the other through an on-line version of the course. Although subjective comments about the experience filled the spectrum, the results on both the mid-term and the final examinations (the only times when the on-line group ever showed up) revealed that "the wired students outscored their traditional counterparts by an average of 20 per cent" (McCollum, 1997, p. A23).

Summary

This section has sought to trace the research pertinent to the study at hand which relates directly to the adoption of an innovation within an educational setting. A brief overview of the landmark work of Rogers (1962) was followed by an analysis of the effects of change at the micro level, that of the individual. The work of Fuller (1969) which served as a basis for the Concerns-Based Adoption Model of Hall et al. (1973) was reviewed. The parts of the CBAM were described in detail, and examples of the incorporation of CBAM into other models also accounting for individual preferences was discussed. Applications of diagnostic frameworks of the CBAM were also presented. Development of the Stages of Concern Questionnaire and its psychometric properties were outlined. Special attention was given to the demographic page which typically accompanies it and to studies which looked at the possible relationships between the variables captured on the demographic page and the stages of concern. Finally, a brief overview of the recent history of the Internet and of its growing contribution to the changes underway in instruction at institutions of higher education was given.

CHAPTER 3
RESEARCH DESIGN

Study Design/Procedures

Of primary interest in this descriptive correlational study are the concerns regarding the innovation adoption of the Internet for instructional purposes among the faculty at the University of Florida. To explore these concerns, the following questions were posed:

(1) What are the relationships of the levels of Internet use for instructional purposes and the levels of Internet use for all other purposes to the sequence of stages of concern?

(2) Are there significant differences in the peak stages of concern of the faculty members grouped by the extent to which they modify their instructional practices based on how or what students learn?

(3) Are there significant differences in the peak stages of concern among faculty members grouped by rank, gender, age, or national origin?

43

Variables

The dependent variable in the study was the peak or most intense of the seven stages of concern about adoption of the Internet for instructional purposes. Derived from the Stages of Concern Questionnaire, each stage score ranges from 0 to 35 on Stage 0-Awareness, Stage 1-Personal, Stage 2-Information, Stage 3-Management, Stage 4-Consequence, Stage 5-Collaboration, and Stage 6-Refocusing.

The independent variables were level of Internet use for instructional purposes, level of Internet use for all other purposes, level of attention paid to how students learn, level of attention paid to what students learn, rank, gender, age, and national origin.

Sample

The population for this study consisted of the 1,650 persons employed at the University of Florida during spring semester 1997 who are remunerated as faculty within the following ten college-level units: Architecture, Business Administration, Education, Engineering, Fine Arts, Health and Human Performance, Health Professions, the Institute of Food and Agricultural Sciences, Journalism and Communications, and Liberal Arts and Sciences. The Office of the Associate Vice-President for Academic Affairs supplied the labels used to distribute the questionnaire to the nine colleges, and the IFAS mailing facility supplied them for that unit.

Since a time lag typically occurs between a) when a faculty member leaves or a new one is appointed and starts to work and b) when the database is updated to reflect the changes, the information from these labels vary slightly from the true number of faculty within an academic unit at any given time.

The Office of Academic Affairs supplies labels pre-addressed with department names and the number of faculty at a given destination according to the latest database figures. When mail is delivered bearing these labels, it is put into faculty mailboxes without regard to the names of the currently employed members. To provide a more complete profile of the respondents and to control for questionnaires destined to those other than the intended, additional demographic data were collected on what percent-time the faculty member was teaching during the semester of the survey, whether the faculty member was working part- or full-time, academic rank and type of faculty line (tenure/non-tenure).

The mailing labels supplied by the mailing facility of the Institute of Food and Agricultural Sciences were personally addressed. These labels were affixed to the top

of the letters of transmittal, and the surveys were grouped
into envelopes by academic unit.

Instrumentation

The instrument used in this mailed survey was the 35-
item Stages of Concern Questionnaire, developed by The
Research and Development Center for Teacher Education at The
University of Texas at Austin as part of the Procedures for
Adopting Educational Innovations/CBAM Project (Hall et al.,
1979). Permission to use the copyrighted questionnaire for
the purpose of this study was requested on October 31, 1996,
and granted on November 1, 1996 (see letter in Appendix B).

The Institutional Review Board of the University of
Florida reviewed a draft of the entire instrument and the
cover letter submitted on December 5, 1996; approval was
granted on December 12, 1996 (see letter in Appendix C).

Development of the questionnaire

The conceptual basis for developing a questionnaire of
concerns about adoption of an innovation grew out of the
extensive work of Frances Fuller during the 1960s and Gene
Hall and his associates during the 1970s. From responses
elicited by an open-ended concerns survey, a total of 544
items was narrowed to a group of 400 judged as central to
measuring concerns. From these, editing and eliminating
redundant items left 195. After administering this 195-item

survey and analyzing the data from 359 respondents, over 60% of the variance in the items was attributed to seven factors, a finding resulting from item correlation and factor analyses. The seven stages of concern represent the outcome of this work (Hall et al., 1979).

Throughout the subsequent testing of the instrument and its eventual shortening to the current 35 items, administration of the survey was on populations of teachers and college faculty involved in adoption of a number of educational innovations. For example, in 1974 (n = 359) the innovation at the higher education level was the use of instructional modules, while that for elementary teachers was teaming (Hall et al., 1979).

Reliability/Validity

Internal reliability (alpha) coefficients for the stages range from .64 to .83 (n = 830, a stratified sample of professors and teachers). Test-retest correlations (n = 132, two weeks elapsed) are from .65 to .86 (Hall et al., 1979, p. 11).

Indications of the validity of the instrument include the correlations between individual items and the stage which they supposedly measure (72% of the items had higher correlations with their assigned stage than with other stages), lower correlations between distant stages than between adjacent ones, results of factor analyses which indicate independence of the individual stage subscales, and multi-method procedures using the survey and interviews resulting in multiple Rs greater than .56 (p < .05) for four of the stages (Hall et al., 1979).

Description of the Questionnaire

Respondents choose from eight alternatives on a Likert-type scale: (0) irrelevant, or one of seven levels of concern (level 1 is defined as "Not true of me now"; levels 2, 3, and 4 represent gradations of "Somewhat true of me now"; and levels 5, 6, and 7 represent gradations of "Very true of me now" [Hall et al., 1979, p. 69]). Each of the seven stage scores is the sum of the five individual item scores measuring that stage of concern, constituting a range of from 0 to 35. A description of each stage and the five items which make up the score for that stage are as follows (adapted from Hall et al., 1979; original concept from Hall et al., 1973):

0 Awareness. Little concern about or involvement with the innovation is indicated.

I don't even know what using the Internet for instructional purposes would be.

I am not concerned about use of the Internet for instructional purposes.

I am completely occupied with other things.

Although I don't know about instructional Internet use,
I am concerned about issues in this area.

At this time, I am not interested in learning about
using the Internet for instructional purposes.

1 Informational. A general awareness of the innovation
and interest in learning more detail about it is indicated.
The person seems to be unworried about himself/herself in
relation to the innovation. S/he is interested in
substantive aspects of the innovation in a selfless manner
such as general characteristics, effects, and requirements
for use.

I have a very limited knowledge of instructional uses
of the Internet.

I would like to discuss the possibility of using the
Internet for instructional purposes.

I would like to know what resources are available if we
decide to adopt instructional use of the Internet.

I would like to know what instructional use of the
Internet will require in the immediate future.

I would like to know how instructional use of the
Internet is better than what we are doing now.

2 Personal. Individual is uncertain about the demands
of the innovation, his/her inadequacy to meet those demands,
and his/her role with the innovation. This includes
analysis of his/her role in relation to the reward

structure of the organization, decision making, and consideration of potential conflicts with existing structures or personal commitment. Financial or status implications of the program for self and colleagues may also be reflected.

I would like to know the effect of using the Internet for instructional purposes on my professional status.

I would like to know who will make the decisions regarding use of the Internet for instruction.

I would like to know how my teaching or administration is supposed to change.

I need more information on time and energy commitments required by instructional Internet use.

I would like to know how my role will change when I am using the Internet for instructional purposes.

3 Management. Attention is focused on the processes and tasks of using the innovation and the best use of information and resources. Issues related to efficiency, organizing, managing, scheduling, and time demands are utmost.

I am concerned about not having enough time to organize myself each day.

I am concerned about conflict between my interests and my responsibilities.

I am concerned about my inability to manage all that instructional Internet use requires.

I am concerned about time spent working with non-academic problems related to using the Internet for instructional purposes.

Coordinating tasks/people takes too much of my time.

4 Consequence. Attention focuses on impact of the innovation on student in his/her immediate sphere of influence. The focus is on relevance of the innovation for students, evaluation of student outcomes, including performance and competencies, and changes needed to increase student outcomes.

I am concerned about students' attitudes toward instructional use of the Internet.

I am concerned about how instructional use of the Internet affects students.

I am concerned about evaluating my impact on students.

I would like to excite my students about their part in using the Internet for instructional purposes.

I would like to use feedback from students to change use of the Internet for instruction.

5 Collaboration. The focus is on coordination and cooperation with others regarding use of the innovation.

I would like to help other faculty in their instructional Internet use.

I would like to develop working relationships with both our faculty and outside faculty using the Internet for instructional purposes.

I would like to familiarize other departments or persons with our progress in using the Internet.

I would like to coordinate my effort with others to maximize the effects of instructional Internet use.

I would like to know what other faculty are doing in this area.

6 Refocusing. The focus is on exploration of more universal benefits from the innovation, including the possibility of major changes or replacement with a more powerful alternative. Individual has definite ideas about alternatives to the proposed or existing form of the innovation.

I now know of some other approaches that might work better.

I am concerned about revising my instructional use of the Internet.

I would like to revise the instructional approach to use of the Internet.

I would like to modify our instructional use of the Internet based on the experiences of our students.

I would like to determine how to supplement, enhance, or replace instructional use of the Internet.

In addition to the responses on the Stages of Concern Questionnaire, data from demographic variables were also collected. The percent time teaching during the semester of inquiry, working part- vs. full-time, and the type of faculty line held (tenure or non-tenure) were collected to control for distribution of the questionnaires to those who do not make up the population of primary interest to the study.

Levels of use of the Internet for instructional purposes and levels of use of the Internet for all other purposes were collected to address research question 1 and to test theory from the Concerns-Based Adoption Model. Stages of concern are the first dimension of the CBAM, and levels of use make up the second dimension. In the CBAM eight different levels of use are proposed. More pro-active in nature, the levels of use sequence resembles that of the stages of concern quite closely, as do the description of the states and the decisions made by the user. The eight levels of use (Hord, et al., 1987, p. 55) and their corresponding stages of concern are:

Level of Use	Stage of Concern
Level 0 Non-Use	Stage 0 Awareness
Level 1 Orientation	Stage 1 Information
Level 2 Preparation	Stage 2 Preparation
Level 3 Mechanical Use	
	Stage 3 Management
Level 4a Routine	
	Stage 4 Consequence
Level 4b Refinement	
Level 5 Integration	Stage 5 Collaboration
Level 6 Renewal	Stage 6 Refocusing

Levels of use are typically determined during a focused interview with the help of an extremely detailed and explicit chart. Since the size of the sample for this study necessitated gathering the data on a survey, a taxonomy appropriate for such a technique had to be found. Dreyfus and Dreyfus (1986) offer the five-stage model for skill acquisition which has been used here. A category for the non-user was added to their five levels as outlined below. The corresponding levels of use from the CBAM are also shown:

CBAM Level of Use	Survey Terms
Level 0 Non-Use	
Level 1 Orientation	Non-user
Level 2 Preparation	
Level 3 Mechanical	Novice

Level 4a Routine	Advanced beginner
Level 4b Refinement	Competent user
Level 5 Integration	Proficient user
Level 6 Renewal	Expert

Finally, items inquiring about the number of years at the institution, length of time involved with instructional use of the Internet, prior formal training in the Internet for instructional purposes, and recent or concurrent involvement in some other major innovation or program were taken from the original demographic variable sheet suggested by Hall, et al. (1979) and contribute to the full assessment of the "state of the user system" (p. 52).

An estimate of the completion time of the 35-item SoCQ was ten to fifteen minutes. The additional items did not add substantially to this range.

The questionnaire was distributed to a panel of six experts, all members of the same group to whom it would eventually be distributed, for comment on overall clarity of the items and suggestions for improvement. The final version reflected the incorporation of their suggestions. In one case the order of the demographic variable items was changed, and response to other comments led to naming 'the Internet for instructional purposes' rather than relying on 'the innovation' throughout (survey found in Appendix D).

Data Collection

The first announcement of the study was mailed on
January 10, 1997, on a bright pink post card. Its primary
objective was to alert the faculty to the coming survey.
The text of the notice is found in Appendix E.

The questionnaire itself was duplicated front and back
on high-quality pink paper and was accompanied by a letter
of transmittal on top. The letter of transmittal was on the
letterhead of the University Center for Excellence in
Teaching and was signed by the director (see Appendix E).
The first page under the letter of transmittal was dedicated
to instructions on filling out the concerns questionnaire.
The format and wording were taken directly from Hall et al.,
1979. Specific definitions of 'Internet' and 'instructional
purpose' were included, as well as examples of the latter.
The survey began on the back of the instructions page.
The questions were numbered consecutively, and the final
page included an area for the respondent to write comments.
The return address was placed on the instruction page,
repeated again at the end of the questionnaire below the
comments area, and printed three times on the final
(outside) page. Respondents were requested to fold, close,
and return the questionnaires via campus mail.

To prepare the questionnaires for mailing, each
academic unit was assigned a three-digit code number, and
that same number was placed on each questionnaire destined
for that academic unit. The number of faculty indicated on
the label determined the number of questionnaires placed in
a large manilla envelope destined for that academic unit. A
cover sheet was included on top requesting the cooperation
of the recipient in distributing the questionnaires to the
faculty for whom they were intended.

The questionnaire itself was sent through campus mail
on Friday of the third week of spring semester, i.e.,
January 24, 1997. The timing of the mailing sought to
maximize the attention it might get among those on an
academic schedule with an uneven workload distribution
throughout the typical sixteen-week semester.

Simultaneous with the mailing, the questionnaire was
posted on the World Wide Web at the UCET site. Care was
taken in the design of the survey for the web site so that
responses would be comparable irrespective of which medium a
respondent used. Although all those who replied had a paper
copy of the questionnaire available to them, they did not
need any information from the paper copy to be able to
answer the form over the Internet. Links to the full text
of the letter of transmittal and to the instructions for

filling out the Stages of Concern Questionnaire were included. At the end of the form the respondent activated a "Send Form" button which transmitted the results to an email address anonymously.

The Internet address for the site was included in the cover letter and repeated on the questionnaire instruction page. The electronic form had one additional demographic item at the beginning; it requested the respondent's departmental affiliation (either the three-digit code from the paper copy or the name of the academic unit), since this information was lost from the paper copy by those choosing to submit their responses electronically.

The requested return date of the instruments was Wednesday, February 5, 1997, or twelve days after they were mailed out.

A follow-up mailing following the same procedure was undertaken. The letter of transmittal included a polite reminder and a request to complete the questionnaire. Those who had already done so were asked to disregard the request (see Appendix F for follow-up letter of transmittal). The mailing of the follow-up went out on Friday, February 21, 1997, and return was requested by Wednesday, March 5, 1997, again an interval of twelve days. This second deadline fell

in the middle of the week immediately prior to the week-long
spring break.

Data Analysis

Responses to the survey from the three mailings totaled
540 of a possible 1,650 in the population. Of these, 50 (or
9%) were received electronically. The sample thus
represents a 33% response rate. This compares favorably
with the results found during a review of the literature for
similar surveys on equivalent populations (response rate
percentages in the high twenties were the rule although one
was found at 32). Furthermore, surveys within the last year
on subsets of this population, one undertaken within the
Institute of Food and Agricultural Sciences only and another
campus-wide of new faculty after their first year at the
University of Florida, had response rates of 20% and 30%
respectively.

The survey data were entered, verified, and saved on a
3.5" disk from where they were subsequently stored on the
mainframe of the University of Florida Center for
Instructional and Research Computing Activities. Analyses
of the data were carried out using SAS run interactively
with the UNIX operating system on the mainframe.

Demographic information on the respondents is shown in Table 1. Comparison of the sample to all faculty as described in the University of Florida Affirmative Action Plan-1996 shows that females are represented only slightly higher in the sample than in the population (26.2% of the sample vs 25.7% of all faculty) and that those on tenure-track faculty lines responded in a higher proportion (85.3% of the sample vs 74.0% of all faculty occupy faculty lines).

In order to address the research questions, a correlational analysis and multiple regression were used. The alpha level to test for statistical significance was set at .05.

Summary

This section has given an overview of the study undertaken, including the design of the study, the variables, the instrument, and the procedures followed. Specifically, the sample is described; the instrument is identified and described, and its development is traced; methods of data collection are outlined; demographic variables are reported for the respondents; and analyses of the data are set out.

Table 1

Demographic Profile of the Respondents

	f	%

Time (N = 531)

Part-time	30	6
Full-time	501	94

Gender (N = 530)

Male	379	72
Female	151	28

Rank (N = 538)

Instructor/Lecturer	34	6
Post-doc	2	0
Assistant Professor	106	20
Associate Professor	138	26
Professor	226	42
Other	32	6

Track (N = 534)

Tenure	456	85
Non-tenure	78	15

National Origin (N = 531)

American	457	86
Foreign	74	14

CHAPTER 4
RESULTS AND DISCUSSION

This sections opens with a restatement of the problem and of the research questions of interest in the study. These are followed by the variables chosen for the study and then a section on the findings. The data are first analyzed descriptively one at a time. Then the bivariate relationships are examined. Finally, the results of the multiple regression analysis of the data are given, specifically in relation to the research questions set out at the beginning of the study. Also included is a discussion of the meaning of each of the significant findings and its relationship to findings of previous studies.

Research Questions

Central to this descriptive correlational study were the concerns regarding the innovation adoption of the Internet for instructional purposes among the faculty at the University of Florida. To explore these concerns, the following questions were posed:

(1) What are the relationships of the levels of

62

Internet use for instructional purposes and the levels of
Internet use for all other purposes to the sequence of
stages of concern?

(2) Are there significant differences in the peak
stages of concern of the faculty members grouped by the
extent to which they modify their instructional practices
based on how or what students learn?

(3) Are there significant differences in the peak
stages of concern among faculty members grouped by rank,
gender, age, or national origin?

Variables

The dependent variable in the study was the peak or
most intense stage of the seven stages of concern about
adoption of the Internet for instructional purposes.
Derived from the Stages of Concern Questionnaire, each stage
score ranges from 0 to 35 on Stage 0-Awareness, Stage 1-
Personal, Stage 2-Information, Stage 3-Management, Stage 4-
Consequence, Stage 5-Collaboration, and Stage 6-Refocusing.
Although all respondents to the questionnaire have scores on
all seven stages of concern, only the peak stage of concern
of each individual was of interest in this study. When two
or more stage of concern scores shared an equal intensity
(i.e., an equal score within the 0-to-35 range), the stage
at the further (furthest) point along the developmental

continuum from Stage 0 to Stage 6 was chosen as the peak stage of concern.

The independent variables were level of Internet use for instructional purposes, level of Internet use for all other purposes, level of attention paid to how students learn, level of attention paid to what students learn, rank, gender, age, and national origin.

In order to address the research questions, the alpha level was set at .05, and a correlational analysis and regression technique were used. Borg and Gall (1989) mention that when dealing with "the degree of relationship among various combinations of three or more variables" multiple regression is a technique offering "considerable versatility" (p. 601) in correlational studies.

Findings

Descriptive Statistics

The greatest portion of the sample, 132 or about one-fourth of the respondents, was found to exhibit their peak stage of concern regarding adoption of the educational innovation of use of the Internet for instructional purposes at the first of the self stages, Information. Another 119 (22%) of the sample were found to be at Stage 4 - Consequence, the first of the impact stages. The mean peak stage of concern for the sample was 2.90 (SD = 1.94) (high Stage 2 - Personal). (See Table 2 for a complete summary.)

Table 3 displays the findings on the levels of use of the sample participants with regard to the Internet. Over half of the sample self-reported a level of use of the Internet for instructional purposes of non-use or novice (n = 349). Levels of use of the Internet for all other purposes, however, were higher. Over two-thirds of the sample use the Internet for non-instructional purposes at the self-reported levels of novice, advanced beginner, or competent user. The mean for instructional use of the Internet fell at level 1 - novice (M = 1.24, SD = 1.33), whereas that for its use for all other purposes fell at level 2 - advanced beginner (M = 2.28, SD = 1.30).

Responses to the survey items asking how much participants modify their teaching on the basis of how and what students learn are shown in Table 4. About 65% (n = 311) of the participants reported that they alter their teaching on the basis of how students learn to an average degree or quite a bit. Likewise 310 members of the sample or 67% reported one of the same two categories when asked about how much they change their teaching according to what students learn.

A profile of the sample respondents with regard to their rank, gender, and national origin is given in Table 5.

Table 2

Peak Stage of Concern

Stage (N = 540)	f	$\%$
0 - Awareness	47	9
1 - Information	132	24
2 - Personal	77	14
3 - Management	53	10
4 - Consequence	119	22
5 - Collaboration	26	5
6 - Refocusing	86	16

Note. M = 2.90.

SD = 1.94.

Table 3

Levels of Use of the Internet

Level	f	%
Instructional purposes (N = 533)		
0 - Non-user	207	39
1 - Novice	142	27
2 - Advanced beginner	81	15
3 - Competent user	67	13
4 - Proficient user	23	4
5 - Expert	13	2
Non-instructional purposes (N = 537)		
0 - Non-user	45	8
1 - Novice	115	21
2 - Advanced beginner	150	28
3 - Competent user	122	23
4 - Proficient user	84	16
5 - Expert	21	4

Note. Instructional purposes: M = 1.24.

SD = 1.33.

Non-instructional purposes: M = 2.28.

SD = 1.30.

Table 4

How Much Teaching Is Modified Based on Student Learning

Degree of Modification	f	%
How students learn (N = 476)		
0 - Not at all	15	3
1 - Moderately	79	17
2 - Average	139	29
3 - Quite a bit	172	36
4 - A great deal	71	15
What students learn (N = 471)		
0 - Not at all	11	2
1 - Moderately	70	15
2 - Average	127	27
3 - Quite a bit	188	40
4 - A great deal	75	16

Note. How: M = 2.43.

SD = 1.03.

What: M = 2.52.

SD = 1.00.

Table 5

Rank, Gender and National Origin of Respondents

Rank (N = 538)	f	%
Instructor/Lecturer	34	6
Post-doc	2	0
Assistant Professor	106	20
Associate Professor	138	26
Professor	226	42
Other	32	6
Gender (N = 530)		
Male	379	72
Female	151	28
National Origin (N = 531)		
American-born	457	86
Foreign-born	74	14

One-fifth of the sample were Assistant Professors, one-fourth (26%) Associate Professors, and just under one-half (42%) were Professors. The sample was about three-fourths male (72%). The age range of the respondents was from 24 to 83 years old; the mean age was 48.58 and the standard deviation was 9.90. The participants were 86% native-born American citizens.

Correlational Relationships

Table 6 contains a correlation matrix showing the zero-order or Pearson product-moment correlations between all the variables in the study. For the purposes of this part of the analysis of the data, the respondents who held a rank other than Assistant Professor, Associate Professor, or Professor were excluded. Lee et al. (1989) state that "no adjustment may be necessary when a very small proportion of cases is excluded" (p. 40)--the case here where 68 of 538, or 12%, were excluded. In addition, the four possible answer choices for the question of whether the respondent was an international faculty member were reduced to a dichotomous variable: American- or foreign-born.

Davis's taxonomy (1971) categorizes the strength of association measured by correlations in the following manner:

Table 6

Intercorrelations Between Peak Stage of Concern and Other Variables

	Peak	L'iip	L'net	How	What	Rank	Sex	Age	Orig
Peak	--								
L'iip	0.33	--							
L'net	0.17	0.65	--						
How	0.10	0.10	-0.05	--					
What	0.02	0.07	0.03	0.57	--				
Rank	-0.05	-0.13	-0.14	-0.18	-0.09	--			
Sex	0.04	-0.15	-0.24	0.17	0.11	-0.32	--		
Age	-0.07	-0.16	-0.25	-0.04	0.01	0.68	-0.18	--	
Orig	0.04	0.02	0.07	0.04	0.09	-0.02	-0.03	0.01	--

Note. Peak = peak stage of concern; L'iip = level of instructional Internet use; L'net = non-instructional Internet use level; How = attention to how students learn; What = attention to what students learn; Orig = national origin (American- or foreign-born). Single underline denotes $p < 0.05$; double underline denotes $p < 0.01$.

Correlation Value	Classification
.70 and above	Very strong
.50 to .69	Substantial
.30 to .49	Moderate
.10 to .29	Low
.01 to .09	Negligible

When the independent variables are viewed one at a time for a relationship to the dependent variable peak stage of concern, three are found to be significantly correlated with the outcome variable. Moderately correlated with peak stage of concern is level of use of the Internet for instructional purposes (r = 0.33, p < .01). Level of use of the Internet for all other purposes is also significantly related to peak stage of concern, but this variable demonstrates only a low level of strength of association (r = 0.17, p < .01) according to Davis's terminology. Finally, degree to which respondents reported that they modify their teaching based on how students learn also showed a low level of strength of association (r = 0.10, p < .05).

Further bivariate analysis of the data included viewing the scatter diagrams to assure that a linear relationship was "a reasonable approximation" (Agresti & Finlay, 1986, p. 274) of the assumed form of the relationships between peak stage of concern and the independent variables. In each case, this assumption was confirmed.

Regression Analysis

Finally, a multiple regression with all of the variables of interest in the study was carried out to determine the contribution of each to the prediction of peak stage of concern when all others were controlled. Results are given in Table 7.

Research Question 1

What are the relationships of the levels of Internet use for instructional purposes and the levels of Internet use for all other purposes to the sequence of stages of concern?

Both levels of use of the Internet for instructional purposes and levels of use of the Internet for all other purposes are significantly correlated with peak stage of concern. However, when controlling for other variables, only level of use of the Internet for instructional purposes has a significant strength of association with peak stage of concern (t = 7.591, p < 0.0001). All other variables being equal, a respondent who was one level higher in use of the Internet for instructional purposes exhibited a peak stage of concern 0.62 stage higher.

Table 7

Summary of Multiple Regression for Variables Predicting Peak
Stage of Concern

Variable	B	SE B
Level of use of the Internet for instructional purposes	0.62*	0.08
Level of use of the Internet for all other purposes	-0.08	0.09
Degree of modification to teaching based on how students learn	0.12	0.11
Degree of modification to teaching based on what students learn	-0.12	0.11
Rank	0.15	0.15
Gender	0.54*	0.21
Age	-0.01	0.01
National Origin	-0.02	0.24

Note. * $p < .05$.

The findings of the significant contribution of level
of use of the educational adoption being investigated in
this study, use of the Internet for instructional purposes,
confirm the theory of the Concerns-Based Adoption Model,
which states that stages of concern about the innovation and
Levels of Use of the same "will move in nearly a one-to-one
correspondence" (Loucks & Hall, 1977, p. 20).

Research Question 2

Are there significant differences in the peak stages of
concern of the faculty members grouped by the extent to
which they modify their instructional practices based on how
or what students learn?

The degree to which participants reported that they
modify their teaching based on how students learn proved to
be significantly correlated to peak stage of concern,
although the degree to which they claimed to modify their
instruction based on what students learn did not.

This finding would lend support to the results of the
1989 study by Leong-Childs, who found that Stanford
University School of Humanities and Sciences professors who
were innovative instructional computer users differed
significantly in the amount of attention they pay to how
their students learn.

Nevertheless, when all other variables of the current study were controlled, neither degree to which respondents modify their teaching based on how students learn nor the same based on what students learn contributed significantly to the prediction of peak stage of concern (t = 1.165 for attention to how students learn and t = -1.125 for attention to what).

Research Question 3

Are there significant differences in the peak stages of concern among faculty members grouped by rank, gender, age, or national origin?

Rank was not significantly correlated to peak stage of concern; and when all other variables were controlled, it did not have a significant strength of association with peak stage of concern (t = 1.024).

Although gender was not significantly correlated to peak stage of concern, when all other variables were controlled it contributed significantly to the prediction of peak stage of concern (t = 2.543, p = 0.0114). When all other variables were controlled, women respondents were predicted to be .54 stage higher on their peak stage of concern.

This finding for the respondents in the sample would seem to refute the results of research reported by Hall et al. (1979) reporting "no outstanding relationships between standard demographic variables and concerns data" (p. 52) and concurring with Rutherford (1986) that gender (and other variables) lack any "consistent relationship" (p. 7) with stage of concern scores.

Age was not significantly correlated to peak stage of concern; and when all other variables were controlled, it did not have a significant strength of association with peak stage of concern (t = .0832). This would validate the findings of Hall et al. (1979) and Rutherford (1986).

National origin was not significantly correlated to peak stage of concern; and when all other variables were controlled, it did not make a significant contribution to the prediction of peak stage of concern (t = -0.071). Although Shoemaker (1990) found significant differences in stage of concern scores about adoption of instructional use of computers in foreign language teaching among the five foreign culture groups (as defined by native language and country of birth) he investigated, his study dealt solely with foreign culture groups. Since Shoemaker's study did not include Americans as a cultural group and the foreign-born respondents of this study were not further subdivided, no direct parallel can be drawn.

CHAPTER 5
SUMMARY AND CONCLUSIONS

This section opens with a summary of the study undertaken. It then moves on to reiterate the findings and to state the conclusions which can be reasonably drawn from those findings. Implications for the conclusions are given, and finally recommendations for further research are outlined.

Summary

This exploratory, descriptive correlational study set out to measure the stages of concern of the faculty of the University of Florida regarding adoption of the innovation of use of the Internet for instructional purposes.

The current paradigm shift underway as institutions of higher education break out of the constraints of the last several hundred years of a model of same time, same place learning has incited exploration of new modes of instructional delivery. Recent advances in computers and telecommunications technology have been crucial to the role the Internet will play in this shift. Greater capacity for storage and faster retrieval and transfer of information

78

have meant greater potential for this medium than could have been conceived of only a short time ago.

Teachers, not unlike others confronted with change or innovation, react in a number of ways to the current times. Some avail themselves of training and informal meetings to learn about what others have done or to share what they have accomplished. A mid-April 1997 talk entitled "Impact of Multimedia Lectures" given by a faculty member of the Department of Psychology at the University of Florida and sponsored by the University Center for Excellence in Teaching and the Office of Instructional Resources resulted in higher attendance than any such voluntary meeting to date. Over 60 faculty members, administrators, and graduate teaching assistants gathered to hear about the experience of one of their colleagues and to learn from it.

The topic addressed at this lecture represents quite a different orientation from that of workshops being given as few as two years ago, where during a one-day conference called Data Day '95 University of Florida officials organized sessions to inform faculty and graduate students about " Internet resources that faculty may not be aware of" (Passarella, 1995, p. 8). At that time a member of the organizing committee admitted to not anticipating a sophisticated level of experience among those attending.

Faculty concerns over instructional use of the Internet have become even more pertinent during the 1996-1997 academic year. As changes in access to computers and networked resources in student computer laboratories across campus have been put into effect, students have resisted paying an additional fee. The administration's distinction between essential and elective computer access has been one with which students could not agree.

The theoretical framework for the study was the Concerns-Based Adoption Model, which has been developed to help facilitate change at the level of the individual involved with innovation adoption within educational settings. The model was developed by Gene Hall and his associates at The Research and Development Center for Teacher Education of the University of Texas at Austin as part of the Procedures for Adopting Educational Innovations/CBAM Project. The model has multiple dimensions which serve to guide change facilitators and others for successful implementation of educational change.

The first dimension of the CBAM involves the stages of concern, further described as seven psychological constructs through which an individual passes when confronted with change. Concerns are defined as an individual's motivation, thoughts, feelings, and perceptions.

The Stages of Concern Questionnaire has been developed to measure an individual's concerns regarding an educational innovation. Interventions designed to resolve the most intense stage(s) of concern are thought to promote more efficient and effective implementation of the innovation being proposed. Moreover, arousal of concerns at higher stages is unlikely until resolution has been achieved at lower stages of concern. The 35-item questionnaire offers a pencil-and-paper measure of an individual's concerns and supplies important information for planning training interventions.

Specifically, the research questions the study set out to answer were:

(1) What are the relationships of the level of Internet use for instructional purposes and the level of Internet use for all other purposes to the sequence of stages of concern?

(2) Are there significant differences in the peak stages of concern of the faculty members grouped by the extent to which they modify their instructional practices based on how or what students learn?

(3) Are there significant differences in the peak stages of concern among faculty members grouped by rank, gender, age, or national origin?

In order to investigate these questions, a mailed survey using the Stages of Concern Questionnaire was carried out of 1,650 faculty members in ten colleges within the University of Florida. A total of 540 responses (33%) provided the data for analyzing the results.

Findings

With respect to the first research question, both levels of use of the Internet for instructional purposes and levels of use for all other purposes were significantly correlated with peak stage of concern among the members of the sample. Nevertheless, when controlling for other variables of interest in the study, only level of use of the Internet for instructional purposes contributes significantly to the prediction of peak stage of concern. Typically, the respondent who was one level of use higher was .62 stage further along in the developmental continuum known as stages of concern.

With regard to the second research question, only the extent to which respondents reported that they change their teaching based on how students learn was significantly correlated to peak stage of concern. When the other variables were controlled, neither the extent to which respondents reported that they change their teaching based on how students learn nor the same based on what students learn showed a significant contribution to prediction of peak stage of concern.

Finally, among the variables of rank, gender, age, and national origin, none was significantly correlated to the outcome variable. Furthermore, only gender exhibited a significant contribution to prediction of peak stage of concern when all other variables were controlled.

Implications

Since instructional use of the Internet is similar to instructional use of other computer technology in that it often has a preceding use which may involve research or even recreation before transfer of the power and potential of the technology to classroom applications, the finding in this study that level of use of the Internet for instructional purposes will significantly contribute to predicting peak stage of concern is not surprising. Promoting use of the Internet for _any_ purpose among university faculty may well spur the user on to recognizing possible teaching applications. In order to increase awareness of what is available, an issue as simple as faculty member access to network connectivity in the office first, and updated equipment with sufficient processing speed and memory capacity second, may well be key among the conditions that would promote instructional applications of this medium. Mention is made of spending future allocations from the technology fee generated by the monies collected from students on connecting every classroom to the Internet. However, this may well be 'buying the saddle before buying the horse.' Attention to assuring that every faculty office is connected first and supplied with sufficient resources to benefit from something so simple and low-tech as email first and then from what is available on the Internet may indeed be a more informed route.

Since gender is correlated negatively with rank (-0.32, p < .01) as well as with age (-0.18, p < .01) in the sample, we know that women tend to be represented more than would be expected at the lower ranks and among the younger faculty members. In addition, gender maintained a significant contribution to the prediction of peak stage of concern when all other variables were controlled. This would mean that controlling for other variables women of the sample tend to be further along the developmental continuum represented by the seven stages of concern (and probably levels of use) regarding adopting the innovation of use of the Internet for instructional purposes. The findings place these young women at the lower ranks in key positions to become change agents for their colleagues.

Recommendations for Further Research

If level of use of the Internet for instructional purposes is associated with reaching a given stage of concern regarding adoption of this educational innovation and, in turn, level of use of the Internet for all other purposes is correlated significantly with its use in the classroom, then further research into the components of its use in both categories is needed. Another topic of interest would be the progression of the interest in and use of the Internet from non-instructional uses such as research or recreation to interest in its teaching and learning applications.

Simply gathering information about the numbers and locations of faculty with networked connectivity which permits Internet access in the office and about those who have the appropriate equipment to make the most of the educational potential of the medium would be of great value in setting systematic goals for implementation of wider faculty use of the Internet for instructional purposes across the campus.

Whether driven by student demand, through gradual coercion from sources in the administration, or from colleagues who are innovators, instructional use of the Internet is an innovation which holds promise of being central to the changing patterns in delivery of instruction by institutions of higher education in the United States and throughout the world for some time to come.

REFERENCES

Agresti, A., & Finlay, B. (1986). Statistical methods for the social sciences (2nd ed.). San Francisco: Dellen.

Albright, M. (1996, February 5). Instructional technology and higher education: Rewards, rights and responsibilities. Keynote address of the Southern Regional Faculty and Instructional Development Consortium, Baton Rouge, LA. (ERIC Document Reproduction Service No. ED 392 412)

Aneke, N. (1996). Teachers' stages of concern about a school-wide educational reform (Doctoral dissertation, Virginia Polytechnic Institute and State University, 1996). Dissertation Abstracts International, 57(3), 934A. (University Microfilms No. 9624162)

Borg, W., & Gall, M. (1989). Educational research (5th ed.). New York: Longman.

Cicchelli, T. (1990). Concerns theory in liberal arts related to preservice education of undergraduate and graduate students. Educational Research Quarterly, 14(4), 41-48.

Cicchelli, T., & Baecher, R. (1987). The use of concerns theory in inservice training for computer education. Computers in Education, 11(2), 85-93.

Cicchelli, T., & Baecher, R. (1990). Theory and practice: Implementing computer technology in a secondary school. (ERIC Document Reproduction Service No. ED 336 059)

Clement, J., & Abrahams, J. (1994). Networking in 1993. Educational Media and Technology Yearbook 1994, 20, 106-119.

Chandler, J. (1994). Stages of concern expressed by selected North Carolina community college faculty and staff about the adoption of institutional effectiveness criteria (Doctoral dissertation, North Carolina State University, 1994). (University Microfilms No. 9425455) Dissertation Abstracts International, 55(4), 843A. (University Microfilms No. 9425455)

Dankel, D., Jr. (1996). The use of the World Wide Web in distance education. Paper presented at Computer Expo 1996, University of Florida, Gainesville, FL.

Davis, J. (1971). Elementary survey analysis. Englewood, NJ: Prentice Hall.

Dreyfus, H., & Dreyfus, S. (1986). Mind over machine: The power of human intuition and expertise in the era of the computer. New York: The Free Press.

Falvo, J. (1990). An analysis of language teachers' concerns regarding new technologies: The case of Minnesota teachers of Spanish assessing satellite video technology to deliver authentic cultural materials (Doctoral dissertation, The University of Nebraska-Lincoln, 1990). Dissertation Abstracts International, 52(3), 827A.

Fuller, F. (1969). Concerns of teachers: A developmental conceptualization. American Educational Research Journal, 6(2), 207-226.

Fuller, F., & Brown, O. (1975). Becoming a teacher. In K. Ryan (Ed.), Teacher education: The seventy-fourth yearbook of the national society for the study of education, Part II (pp. 25-52). Chicago: The University of Chicago Press.

Green, K. (1996). Campus computing 1995. Encino, CA: Campus Computing. (ERIC Document Reproduction Service No. ED 394 383)

Hall, G. (1976). The study of individual teacher and professor concerns about innovations. Journal of Teacher Education, 27(1), 22-23.

Hall, G. (1979). The concerns-based approach to facilitating change. Educational Horizons, 57(4), 202-208.

Hall, G. (1985). A stages of concern approach to teacher preparation (Report 3213). Austin, TX: The Research and Development Center for Teacher Education. (ERIC Document Reproduction Service No. ED 265 126)

Hall, G., George, A., & Rutherford, W. (1977). Measuring stages of concern about the innovation: A manual for use of the stages of concern questionnaire. (ERIC Document Reproduction Service No. ED 147 342)

Hall, G., George, A., & Rutherford, W. (1979). Measuring stages of concern about the innovation: A manual for use of the stages of concern questionnaire. (R & D Report No. 3032). Austin, TX: The Research and Development Center for Teacher Education.

Hall, G., & Hord, S. (1987). Change in schools: Facilitating the process. Albany, NY: SUNY Press.

Hall, G., & Loucks, S. (1978). Teacher concerns as a basis for facilitating and personalizing staff development. Teachers College Record, 80(1), 36-53.

Hall, G., & Loucks, S. (1981). Program definition and adaptation: Implications for inservice. Journal of Research and Development in Education, 14(2), 46-58.

Hall, G., & Loucks, S., Rutherford, W., & Newlove, B. (1975). Levels of use of the innovation: A framework for analyzing innovation adoption. Journal of Teacher Education, 26(1), 52-56.

Hall, G., Newlove, B., George, A., Rutherford, W., & Hord, S. (1991). Measuring change facilitator stages of concern--A manual for the use of the CFSoC questionnaire. Greeley, CO: Center for Research on Teaching and Learning, University of Northern Colorado. (ERIC Document Reproduction Service No. ED 353 307)

Hall, G., & Rutherford, W. (1976). Concerns of teachers about implementing team teaching. Educational Leadership, 34(3), 227-233.

Hall, G., Wallace, R., Jr., & Dossett, W. (1973). A developmental conceptualization of the adoption process within educational institutions. Austin, TX: The Research and Development Center for Teacher Education. (ERIC Document Reproduction Service No. ED 095 126)

Hickox, C. (1994). Training for the Internet: Stages of concern among academic library staff in the Amigos Consortium (Doctoral dissertation, East Texas State University, 1994). Dissertation Abstracts International, 55(11), 3383A. (University Microfilms No. 9510955)

Hord, S., & Loucks, S. (1980). A concerns-based model for the delivery of inservice. (ERIC Document Reproduction Service No. ED 206 620)

Hord, S., Rutherford, W., Huling-Austin, L., & Hall, G. (1987). Taking charge of change. Alexandria, VA: Association for Supervision and Curriculum Development.

King, K. (1990). Information technologies in support of teaching and learning. Higher Education Management, 2(3), 294-298.

Kugel, P. (1993). How professors develop as teachers. Studies in Higher Education, 18(3), 315-328.

Lee, E., Forthoffer, R., & Lorimer, R. (1989). Analyzing Complex Survey Data. Newbury Park, CA: Sage.

Lee-Kang, D. (1993). Factors affecting the adoption of instructional use of computers in undergraduate textiles, clothing, and merchandising programs (Doctoral dissertation, The Ohio State University, 1993). Dissertation Abstracts International, 54(11), 4009A. (University Microfilms No. 9412003)

Leong-Childs, D. (1989). Professors' use of computers for innovative instruction (Doctoral dissertation, Stanford University, 1989). Dissertation Abstracts International, 50(7), 1961A. (University Microfilms No. 8925907)

Lewis, D. (1994). Concerns and characteristics affecting the adoption of computer based instruction by diabetes educators (Doctoral dissertation, West Virginia University, 1994). Dissertation Abstracts International, 55(6), 1535A. (University Microfilms No. 9427972)

Loucks, S., & Hall, G. (1977). Assessing and facilitating the implementation of innovations: A new approach. Educational Technology, 17(2), 18-21.

Maddux, C. (1994). The Internet: Educational prospects and problems. Educational Technology, 34(7), 37-42.

Malernee, J. (1997, January 27). Regents approve tuition increase, $50 technology fee. The Independent Florida Alligator, pp. 1, 5.

Marsh, D., & Penn, D. (1988). Engaging students in innovative instruction: An application of the stages of concern framework to studying student engagement. Journal of Classroom Interaction, 23(1), 8-14.

Matthews, R. (1993). Using concerns data to design a staff development program. Journal of Staff Development, 14(3), 52-55.

McCarthy, B. (1982). Improving staff development through CBAM and 4mat. Educational Leadership, 40(1), 20-25.

McCollum, K. (1997, February 21). A professor divides his class in two to test value of on-line instruction. The Chronicle of Higher Education, p. A23.

McQuain, G. (1995). A study examining teacher concerns regarding the implementation of technical preparation programs in the Blue Ridge Community College Service Area. (Doctoral dissertation, University of Virginia, 1995). Dissertation Abstracts International, 56(4), 1224A. (University Microfilms No. 9525968)

Oblinger, D. (1992). Understanding the Internet. (ERIC Document Reproduction Service No. ED 358 861)

Passarella, M. (1995, March 14). UF workshops to teach basic on-line skills. The Independent Florida Alligator, p. 8.

Rogers, E. 1962. Diffusion of innovations. New York: The Free Press.

Rouzie, A. (1995). The new computers and writing course at the University of Texas at Austin: Context and theory. (ERIC Document Reproduction Service No. ED 384 895)

Rudenstine, N. (1997, February 21). The Internet and education: A close fit. The Chronicle of Higher Education, 43(24), p. A48.

Rutherford, W. (1986) Teachers' contributions to school improvement: Reflections on fifteen years of research. (ERIC Document Reproduction Service No. ED 271 462)

Salant, P. (1994). How to conduct your own survey. New York: Wiley.

Schwartz, S. (1996, November). Good ideas for teaching large classes. Innovator, 2(3), 2.

Shehan, C. (1994). The mission of the University Center for Excellence in Teaching. CLAS Notes, 8(8).

Shehan, C. (1995, Fall). The UCET mission. Innovator, 1, 4.

Shoemaker, C. (1990). A study of culture as a determinant in the acceptance of innovative instructional computer use in foreign language instruction for adults (Doctoral dissertation, University of San Francisco, 1990). Dissertation Abstracts International, 51(7), 2242A.

Smith, R. (1995). Teaching physics on line. American Journal of Physics, 63(12), 1090-1096.

Warnock, J. (1996). Exploring education's digital toolkit for the 21st century. Syllabus, 10(4), 14, 16, 37.

Wedman, J., & Strathe, M. (1985). Faculty development in technology: A model for higher education. Educational Technology, 25(2), 15-19.

Wells, J., & Anderson, D. (1995). Teachers' stages of concern toward Internet integration. (ERIC Document Reproduction Service No. ED 389261)

Yessayan, S. (1991). A study of the adaptation to technological innovation in higher education (Doctoral dissertation, The Ohio State University, 1991). Dissertation Abstracts International, 52(2), 518A.

APPENDIX A
STUDENT SENATE PRESIDENT'S LETTER TO ALL UF FACULTY

UNIVERSITY OF FLORIDA

Office of the Senate President

300-54 JWRU
PO Box 118505
Gainesville, FL 32611-8505
(352) 392-1665, ext. 308
Fax: (352) 392-8072

November 19, 1996

To All University of Florida Faculty:

As you may be aware, CIRCA has recently implemented a $20.00 fee to students for the use of computers. The University of Florida Student Senate, representing the university's 40,000 students, finds this policy unacceptable. We are asking for your help in providing students access to computers and the Internet in their educational endeavors.

The attached Student Body Resolution 96-107 was passed unanimously by the Student Senate on October 29, 1996. The resolution gives the "statement of purpose and mission" for the State University System as stated in Florida Statutes 240.105 as well as the "Institutional Purpose" stated in the 1996-97 University Catalog. The costs of all essential elements of fulfilling these purposes are provided through a combination of State Revenues and Student Tuition.

The students of the University of Florida see the use of computers as an *essential*, rather than *elective*, element of fulfilling educational goals. For this reason, we are asking each faculty member to include the following on the syllabi for all courses they teach:.

> **It is the formal policy of this class that in order to fully and properly fulfill the requirements of this course some use of and proficiency in the use of computers, including access to and use of the Internet (e-mail and World Wide Web), will be required.**

With your help in requiring the use of computers for educational purposes, we hope CIRCA will discontinue this policy of charging students for computer use, and address other means of meeting their financial needs.

The student body thanks you for your cooperation in this effort. If you have questions, or would like further information, please contact the Student Senate office. You may e-mail me directly at senpres@sg.ufl.edu.

Sincerely,

Christopher E. Dorworth
Student Senate President

attachment: SBR96-107

Student Senate

300-54 JWRU
PO Box 118505
Gainesville, FL 32611-8505
(352) 392-1665, ext. 308
Fax: (352) 392-8072

Student Body Resolution: 96-107

We, the students of the University of Florida, hereby resolve:

TITLE: Student Body Opposition to Charges for Access to Computing Facilities and
Request for Faculty to Formally Declare Computer Access as Essential

AUTHOR: Charles Grapski
Chris Dorworth, Student Senate President

WHEREAS: Student Government is established for the express purpose, as set forth in the
preamble to the Constitution, to:
1. "Develop better educational standards, facilities, and teaching methods;"
2. "Provide a forum for the expressions of student views and interests;"
3. "Maintain ... academic responsibility, and student rights;"
4. "Foster the recognition of the rights and responsibilities of students to the school, the
community, and humanity;"

AND WHEREAS: The University of Florida publicly states in its official 1996-97 Catalog in reference
to its "Institutional Purpose" that the faculty and staff are dedicated to teaching which the University
declares to be the "fundamental purpose of the university;"

AND WHEREAS: The University of Florida publicly states in its official 1996-97 Catalog in reference
to its "Mission and Goals" that its main goal is "[t]he formation of educated people, the transformation of
mind through learning and the launching of a lifetime of intellectual growth;"

AND WHEREAS: The University of Florida publicly states in its official 1996-97 Catalog in reference
to its "Mission and Goals" that it is "a major, public, comprehensive, land-grant, research university;"

AND WHEREAS: The University of Florida publicly states in its official 1996-97 Catalog in reference
to its "Programs," through numerous citations of its public standing in the academic world, that it is
among the best institutions of higher education in the United States. Additionally the University claims
that "UF is one of the nation's top three universities;"

AND WHEREAS: The State of Florida publicly sets forth in 240.105 Florida Statutes its "Statement of
purpose and mission" for the State University System and its member institutions that:

"(1) The Legislature finds it in the public interest to provide a system of higher education which
is of the highest possible quality; which enables students of all ages, backgrounds, and levels of
income to participate in the search for knowledge and individual development; which stresses
undergraduate teaching as its main priority; which offers selected professional, graduate, and
research programs with emphasis on state and national needs; which fosters diversity of
educational opportunity; which promotes service to the public; which makes effective and
efficient use of human and physical resources; which functions cooperatively with other
educational institutions and systems; and which promotes internal coordination and the wisest
possible use of resources.

(2) The mission of the state system of postsecondary education is to develop human resources, to
discover and disseminate knowledge, to extend knowledge and its application beyond the
boundaries of its campuses, and to serve and stimulate society by developing in students
heightened intellectual, cultural, and humane sensitivities; scientific, professional, and

THEREFORE BE IT RESOLVED: That the Student Senate, as representative of the Student Body, formally declares its opposition to the "elective access" policy implemented on behalf of the University of Florida by CIRCA.

BE IT FURTHER RESOLVED: That the Student Body formally states that it believes that, as an *essential* component of the educational process, access to these computers and computing facilities has already been paid for through State Revenues and Tuition.

BE IT FURTHER RESOLVED: That through the assessment of additional tuition charges through the differential tuition program the Student Body of the University of Florida has directly paid for access to the computers and computing facilities controlled by CIRCA beyond the *essential* level of access.

BE IT FURTHER RESOLVED: That the Student Body reasserts with vigor that access to computers and computing facilities, including but not limited to the use of software packages such as word processing, spreadsheets, databases and access to the Internet, including access to e-mail and the World Wide Web are essential:

AND BE IT FURTHER RESOLVED: That the Student Body requests that all members of the University of Florida faculty formally insert the following lines into all future syllabi, or something to this effect, as well as amend the current syllabi for all courses they teach:

> **It is the formal policy of this class that in order to fully and properly fulfill the requirements of this course some use of and proficiency in the use of computers, including access to and use of the Internet (e-mail and World Wide Web), will be required.**

By formally declaring the necessary and essential nature of such access and officially submitting it to the Director of CIRCA, according to CIRCA's publicly stated policy regarding "elective access" to computers, all students enrolled in those classes shall be granted access to UF's computers and computing facilities at no additional cost for that semester.

Copies to:

University President
University Vice President
Student Body President
Student Body Vice President
Student Body Treasurer
Student Honor Court

Passed 10/29/96
SBR 96-107

Signature:

Christopher E. Dorworth   Date   10/30/96
Student Senate President

APPENDIX B
PERMISSION TO USE STAGES OF CONCERN QUESTIONNAIRE

COLLEGE OF EDUCATION

THE UNIVERSITY OF TEXAS AT AUSTIN

Office of the Dean · George I. Sánchez Building 210 · Austin, Texas 78712
(512) 471-7255 · FAX (512) 471-0846

November 1, 1996

Constance L. Shehan, Ph.D.
Director and Professor of Sociology
University of Florida
109 Rolfs Hall
P.O. Box 112030
Gainesville, FL   32611-2030

Dear Dr. Shehan:

I write in response to your request of October 31, 1996. On behalf of
the copyright holder, The University of Texas at Austin College of
Education grants you permission to use the "Stages of Concern
Questionnaire". This publication was prepared as an activity of the
University's Center for Research and Development in Teacher
Education. The Center lost their federal funding over eight years ago
and is no longer in operation.

With regard to credits, please include the appropriate copyright
notice (Center for Research and Development in Teacher Education,
University of Texas at Austin) on duplicates of the instruments and
otherwise use the credit format standard for academic publications.

Sincerely,

Rosalind Lee
Administrative Associate

rl

APPENDIX C
INSTITUTIONAL REVIEW BOARD APPROVAL

UNIVERSITY OF FLORIDA

114 Psychology Bldg.
PO Box 112250
Gainesville, FL 32611-2250
Phone: (352) 392-0433
Fax: (352) 392-0433

December 12, 1996

TO: Sue Anne Toms
           2402 NRN

FROM: C. Michael Levy, Chair:
          University of Florida Institutional
          Review Board

SUBJECT: Approval of Project #96.613
           Instructional use of the internet: stages of concern among UF
           faculty
           Funding: Unfunded

I am pleased to advise you that the University of Florida Institutional
Review Board has recommended approval of this project. Based on its
review of your protocol, the UFIRB determined that this research presents
no more than minimal risk to participants and, based on 45 CFR 46.117(c),
authorizes you to administer the informed consent process as specified in
the attached description.

If you wish to make any changes in this protocol, you must disclose your
plans before you implement them so that the Board can assess their impact
on your project. In addition, you must report to the Board any unexpected
complications arising from the project which affect your participants.

If you have not completed this project by December 11, 1997, please telephone
our office (392-0433) and we will tell you how to obtain a renewal.

It is important that you keep your Department Chair informed about the status
of this research project.

CML/h2

cc: Vice President for Research
    Dr. Clemens Hallman

APPENDIX D
STAGES OF CONCERN QUESTIONNAIRE

CONCERNS QUESTIONNAIRE

The purpose of this questionnaire is to determine what people who are using or thinking about using the Internet for instructional purposes are concerned about at various times during the innovation adoption process. The items were developed from typical responses of university and school teachers who ranged from no knowledge at all about various innovations to many years experience in using them. Therefore, a good part of the items may appear to be of little relevance or irrelevant to you at this time. For the completely irrelevant items, please circle "0" on the scale. Other items will represent those concerns you do have, in varying degrees of intensity, and should be marked higher on the scale.

            For example: This statement is:

0   1   2   3   4   5   6 (7)   very true of me now.

0   1   2   3 (4) 5   6   7   somewhat true of me at this time.

0 (1) 2   3   4   5   6   7   not at all true of me now.

(0) 1   2   3   4   5   6   7   irrelevant to me.

Please respond to the items in terms of your present concerns, or how you feel about your involvement or potential involvement with use of the INTERNET for instructional purposes. The following definitions will be used:

Internet-the international network linking smaller networks providing access to information (text/graphics/audio/video) throughout those networks and capabilities for electronic mail and file transfer.

Instructional purpose-a use (either required or optional) to support classroom routines, e.g., course announcements, distributing hand-outs, sending or receiving assignments, research for term projects.

Your participation in responding to this questionnaire is both voluntary and anonymous. Please do not write your name anywhere on it.
Thank you for taking time to complete this task by Friday, March 5, 1997. If you prefer, you may respond on-line by going to the form at <http://www.ucet.ufl.edu/internet.html>. Alternatively, you can fax the completed document to 846-1576 or return it folded and closed via campus mail to:
University Center for Excellence in Teaching
P.O. Box 112030

                              Please continue on back --->

Procedures for Adopting Educational Innovations/CBAM Project
R&D Center for Teacher Education, University of Texas at Austin
Copyright, 1974. Reprinted with permission.

101

PLEASE TELL US ABOUT YOURSELF:

1. _____% What percent time are you teaching this semester?

2. Are you working
   0. Part-time
   1. Full-time

3. What is your gender?
   0. Male
   1. Female

4. _____ How old are you?

5. What is your rank?
   0. Instructor/Lecturer
   1. Post-doc
   2. Assistant Professor
   3. Associate Professor
   4. Professor
   5. Other (please specify) _____

6. Which type of faculty line are you on?
   0. Tenure track
   1. Non-tenure track

7. _____ How many years (incl. this one) have you been on the UF faculty?

8. Are you an international faculty member?
   0. I am a native-born U.S. citizen.
   1. I am a naturalized U.S. citizen.
   2. I am a permanent U.S. resident.
   3. I am here on a visa.

9. How long have you been involved with instructional use of the Internet?
   0. Never
   _____ years

10. Using the Internet for instructional purposes, do you consider yourself
    0. a non-user
    1. a novice
    2. an advanced beginner
    3. a competent user
    4. a proficient user
    5. an expert

11. Using the Internet for all other purposes, are you
    0. a non-user
    1. a novice
    2. an advanced beginner
    3. a competent user
    4. a proficient user
    5. an expert

12. Have you had formal training in the Internet for instructional purposes?
    0. No
    1. Yes

13. Are you currently in the first or second year of use of some other major
    innovation or program?
    0. No
    1. Yes

14. How much do you modify your teaching based on **what** students learn?
    0. Not at all
    1. Moderately
    2. Average
    3. Quite a bit
    4. A great deal

15. How much do you modify your teaching based on **how** students learn?
    0. Not at all
    1. Moderately
    2. Average
    3. Quite a bit
    4. A great deal

NOW, PLEASE TELL US WHAT YOU ARE CONCERNED ABOUT:

0	1	2	3	4	5	6	7
Irrelevant	Not true	Somewhat	true	of me now	Very true of me now		

0 1 2 3 4 5 6 7   (16) I am concerned about students' attitudes toward
                       instructional uses of the Internet.

0 1 2 3 4 5 6 7   (17) I now know of some other approaches that might work
                       better.

0 1 2 3 4 5 6 7   (18) I don't even know what using the Internet for
                       instructional purposes would be.

0 1 2 3 4 5 6 7   (19) I am concerned about not having enough time to
                       organize myself each day.

0 1 2 3 4 5 6 7   (20) I would like to help other faculty in their
                       instructional Internet use.

0 1 2 3 4 5 6 7   (21) I have a very limited knowledge of instructional uses
                       of the Internet.

0 1 2 3 4 5 6 7   (22) I would like to know the effect of using the Internet
                       for instructional purposes on my professional status.

0 1 2 3 4 5 6 7   (23) I am concerned about conflict between my interests and
                       my responsibilities.

0 1 2 3 4 5 6 7   (24) I am concerned about revising my instructional use of
                       the Internet.

0 1 2 3 4 5 6 7   (25) I would like to develop working relationships with
                       both our faculty and outside faculty using the
                       Internet for instructional purposes.

0	1	2	3	4	5	6	7
Irrelevant	Not true	Somewhat true of me now			Very true of me now		

0 1 2 3 4 5 6 7 (26) I am concerned about how instructional use of the Internet affects students.

0 1 2 3 4 5 6 7 (27) I am not concerned about use of the Internet for instructional purposes.

0 1 2 3 4 5 6 7 (28) I would like to know who will make the decisions regarding use of the Internet for instruction.

0 1 2 3 4 5 6 7 (29) I would like to discuss the possibility of using the Internet for instructional purposes.

0 1 2 3 4 5 6 7 (30) I would like to know what resources are available if we decide to adopt instructional use of the Internet.

0 1 2 3 4 5 6 7 (31) I am concerned about my inability to manage all that instructional Internet use requires.

0 1 2 3 4 5 6 7 (32) I would like to know how my teaching or administration is supposed to change.

0 1 2 3 4 5 6 7 (33) I would like to familiarize other departments or persons with our progress in using the Internet.

0 1 2 3 4 5 6 7 (34) I am concerned about evaluating my impact on students.

0 1 2 3 4 5 6 7 (35) I would like to revise the instructional approach to use of the Internet.

0 1 2 3 4 5 6 7 (36) I am completely occupied with other things.

0 1 2 3 4 5 6 7 (37) I would like to modify our instructional use of the Internet based on the experiences of our students.

0 1 2 3 4 5 6 7 (38) Although I don't know about instructional Internet use, I am concerned about issues in this area.

0 1 2 3 4 5 6 7 (39) I would like to excite my students about their part in using the Internet for instructional purposes.

0 1 2 3 4 5 6 7 (40) I am concerned about time spent working with non-academic problems related to using the Internet for instructional purposes.

0 1 2 3 4 5 6 7 (41) I would like to know what instructional use of the Internet will require in the immediate future.

0 1 2 3 4 5 6 7 (42) I would like to coordinate my effort with others to maximize the effects of instructional Internet use.

0 1 2 3 4 5 6 7 (43) I need more information on time and energy commitments required by instructional Internet use.

0	1	2	3	4	5	6	7
Irrelevant	Not true	Somewhat true of me now			Very true of me now		

0 1 2 3 4 5 6 7   (44) I would like to know what other faculty are doing in this area.

0 1 2 3 4 5 6 7   (45) At this time, I am not interested in learning about using the Internet for instructional purposes.

0 1 2 3 4 5 6 7   (46) I would like to determine how to supplement, enhance, or replace instructional use of the Internet.

0 1 2 3 4 5 6 7   (47) I would like to use feedback from students to change use of the Internet for instruction.

0 1 2 3 4 5 6 7   (48) I would like to know how my role will change when I am using the Internet for instructional purposes.

0 1 2 3 4 5 6 7   (49) Coordinating tasks/people takes too much of my time.

0 1 2 3 4 5 6 7   (50) I would like to know how instructional use of the Internet is better than what we are doing now.

Your comments will be appreciated.

Thank you for your help. Please fold, close, and return.

University Center for Excellence in Teaching
P.O. Box 112030

TEXT OF INITIAL SURVEY MAILING

Dear UF Faculty Member,

The University Center for Excellence in Teaching is working to improve teaching and learning at the University of Florida. Accurate information about current practices and future needs is essential to this effort. As a faculty member you are asked to contribute to its success.

Within the next week you will receive a questionnaire in campus mail about use of the Internet for instructional purposes. Please take a few minutes to complete the questionnaire as soon as it arrives. Your information will be valuable in helping UCET as it works to improve teaching and learning at the University of Florida.

Sincerely,
Constance L. Shehan, Ph.D.
Director

APPENDIX F
LETTER OF TRANSMITTAL: FIRST MAILING OF QUESTIONNAIRE

UNIVERSITY OF FLORIDA

University Center for Excellence in Teaching

109 Rolfs Hall
PO Box 112030
Gainesville, FL 32611-2030
(904) 846-1574 Fax (904) 846-1576

New Area Code: 352

January 23, 1997

The University Center for Excellence in Teaching is undertaking a survey to collect data on faculty development concerns and needs for use in programming its activities in the coming years.

As a member of the faculty during Spring Semester 1997, your input is essential. Please complete the enclosed questionnaire. Estimated time required is 15 minutes.

Your participation in responding to this questionnaire is both voluntary and anonymous. You do not have to answer any questions you do not wish to answer. Please do not write your name anywhere. The questionnaire has a departmental identification number to enable recording the number of responses by department.

If you prefer, you may respond to the questionnaire on-line and submit your answers anonymously by going to the form on the UCET web site at <http://www.ucet.ufl.edu/internet.html>. Alternatively, you may fax the completed document to 846-1576 or return it folded and closed via campus mail to UCET, P.O. Box 112030. We are requesting responses by Wednesday, February 5, 1997.

If you have any questions about this study, please feel free to email the center at <shehan@soc.ufl.edu> or call 846-1574.

Thank you for your participation. We look forward to your input.

Sincerely,

Constance L. Shehan
Director

APPENDIX G
LETTER OF TRANSMITTAL: FOLLOW-UP MAILING OF QUESTIONNAIRE

UNIVERSITY OF FLORIDA

University Center for Excellence in Teaching

109 Rolfs Hall
PO Box 112030
Gainesville Fl 32611-2030
(352) 846-1574 Fax (352) 846-1576

February 21, 1997

About a month ago we mailed you a questionnaire for the study
of faculty concerns and development needs, especially in
relation to instructional use of the Internet. In case the
first copy was lost, we have enclosed another with this
letter.

Your response will contribute to the success of the project.
Please complete and return the questionnaire by Friday, March
7, 1997. If you would like to respond to the on-line version,
you may do so at

        http://www.ucet.ufl.edu/internet.html

Your response in this study is voluntary and anonymous; you do
not need to answer any questions you do not want to.

Thank you very much for your cooperation and support. If you
have recently returned the questionnaire, please disregard
this letter.

Sincerely,

Constance L. Shehan
Director

BIOGRAPHICAL SKETCH

Sue Anne Toms was born in Mansfield, Ohio, and grew up in Columbus where she attended The Ohio State University and earned a Bachelor of Science degree in education. She also holds a Master of Arts in English as a foreign language from Southern Illinois University. A speaker of eight languages, she has traveled to over 75 countries, studied in Mexico, and lived and worked in Spain, Poland, Puerto Rico, the People's Republic of China, and Thailand. She has held two Fulbrights, one in (the former) Yugoslavia and the other in India. She has been on the faculty of Southern Illinois University, The Pontifical Catholic University of Puerto Rico, and The Ohio State University. She is married to T.C. Chotigeat, and they make their home in Thibodaux, Louisiana.

I certify that I have read this study and that in my opinion it conforms to acceptable standards of scholarly presentation and is fully adequate, in scope and quality, as a dissertation for the degree of Doctor of Philosophy.

Clemens L. Hallman, Chair
Professor of Instruction and Curriculum

I certify that I have read this study and that in my opinion it conforms to acceptable standards of scholarly presentation and is fully adequate, in scope and quality, as a dissertation for the degree of Doctor of Philosophy.

James J. Algina
Professor of Foundations of Education

I certify that I have read this study and that in my opinion it conforms to acceptable standards of scholarly presentation and is fully adequate, in scope and quality, as a dissertation for the degree of Doctor of Philosophy.

Richard D. Downie
Lecturer of Counselor Education

I certify that I have read this study and that in my opinion it conforms to acceptable standards of scholarly presentation and is fully adequate, in scope and quality, as a dissertation for the degree of Doctor of Philosophy.

Sebastian L. Foti
Assistant Professor of Instruction
and Curriculum

This dissertation was submitted to the Graduate Faculty of the College of Education and to the Graduate School and was accepted as partial fulfillment of the requirements for the degree of Doctor of Philosophy.

August 1997

Roderick J. McDavis
Dean, College of Education

_____
Dean, Graduate School

CPSIA information can be obtained
at www.ICGtesting.com
Printed in the USA
BVHW052116090619

550552BV00002B/61/P